C000085400

British Railways in 1948

SPOTLIGHT ON BR

BRITISH RAILWAYS 1948 - 1998
Success or disaster?

Colin Boocock

STATION CAFE

Contents

Title page: BR standard 'Clan' Pacific No. 72001 *Clan Cameron* heads a Glasgow-bound express up Shap incline on 26th June 1957. The train is banked by Fowler 2-6-4T No. 42424. Opinions varied over whether a 4-6-2 of power class 6 ought to have been able to take such loads unaided. *Colour-Rail*

Frontispiece: Resplendent in BR's new "large logo" livery, class 47 Co-Co Brush/Sulzer diesel electric No. 47712 *Lady Diana Spencer* awaits departure from Glasgow Queen Street with the 12.30 push-pull train to Edinburgh Waverley. These trains of mark 3 stock used specially converted mark 2f coaches as driving trailers to control class 47/7 locomotives through a time-division-multiplex system using the train lighting wires.

This page: The decision by the British Steel Corporation to switch from Northampton-mined iron ore to higher grade imported ore was for smelting efficiency reasons and led to shorter ore transits. Thus scenes like this belong to the past. BR standard class 9F 2-10-0 No. 92133 takes a loaded train of ore tipplers through Wellingborough on its way to Scunthorpe on 19th April 1963.

Atlantic Transport Publishers,
Trevithick House, West End, Penryn, Cornwall, TR10 8HE

First Published 1998
© Colin Boocock 1998
ISBN 0 906899 98 2

Layout & Design: Elizabeth Rodriguez & Richard Joy, Paris
Reproduction: Barnabus Design & Repro, Truro, Cornwall
Printed by The Amadeus Press Ltd, Huddersfield, West Yorkshire

Photographs: All photographs in this book were taken by the author except for those that are credited otherwise.
Graphs: The graphs and chart included in this book are intended to illustrate trends during BR's 50 years of existence. They have mostly been produced from data extracted from the BTC and BR annual reports, accounts and statistics. (All these documents are available for public inspection at the Public Record Office, Kew, Surrey.) The bases of financial accounting and statistics produced by the BTC and BR changed several times during the 50 years, as indeed did BR's activities. The author has taken account of the more significant of these changes as far as practicable to ensure fair comparisons one year with another.

All rights reserved. No part of this publication may be reproduced, stored in a retrieval system, or transmitted in any form or by any means, electronic, mechanical, photocopying, recording or otherwise, without prior permission from the publishers.

British Cataloguing in Publication Data: A catalogue record for this book is available from the British Library.

Dedication: The author enjoyed over forty-one years working for the railways in this country, most of them with British Railways plus about eighteen months with Railtrack. The satisfaction of his railway career was enhanced by friendships made with railwaymen of all kinds, by those who helped him and supported the changes he was able to make, and even by those who at times felt it right to oppose those changes. All earned the author's respect and many his admiration for their dedication to their work, a feature that has often been recorded about railway people. This book is dedicated to everyone who made it his or her task to improve their bit of British Railways at any time between 1948 and 1998. **CPB**

ntroduction

ubilee

he inspiration for this book arose from
vo quite dissociated events. The initial
sion was for an album of railway
hotographs that illustrated the progress
at British Railways had made during the
rst fifty years of its existence. BR reached
s Jubilee on 1st January 1998.
rivatisation is complete, and it is timely to
ok back at what has been achieved. The
xt would be mainly narrative, describing
e events that formulated the history and
evelopment of Britain's largest railway
rganisation ever to exist.

A chance remark by a British prime minister
led me to focus the book differently. John
Major, pressed to defend the reasoning
behind the 1992-1997 Conservative
government's intention to privatise the railways of Britain, described British Rail as,
and I quote, "deeply inefficient". I have to
say I felt somewhat hurt by that description.
I had been a full-time railwayman from
1954 to 1996. I had grown up and then
worked on the railways during most of the
events described in this book. There were
indeed many times when the railways were
clearly not efficient. But I believed honestly
that in more recent years our railways had
made substantial progress towards continuously improving their efficiency, however
you measure it. The term "deeply inefficient" did not ring true with me when it
became a Conservative buzz-word in 1996.
Therefore, this book has given me an

opportunity to identify the key changes
and challenges that have faced British
Railways at different times in the past fifty
years, and to review BR's responses to
them. I have questioned the actions taken
to meet each new situation, and have
asked whether the end result in each case
led to greater or lesser "efficiency".
Readers may make up their own minds
from the debates tabled in this book.

Below: During Dr. Beeching's studies in
the early 1960s, the running of extra
summer Saturday trains for holidaymakers
proved to be an uneconomic use of
resources, particularly of older coaching
stock such as the typical GWR vehicles seen
here. On 6th April 1957, former GWR
4-6-0 No. 4077 *Chepstow Castle* pulls into
Bristol Temple Meads station with the
7.50am from Newquay to Manchester.

Right: BR inherited many minor railway by-ways, among the oldest and strangest of which was the Cromford & High Peak line in Derbyshire. This used two rope-worked inclines to move loaded limestone wagons down very steep gradients to reach the Midland main line at Cromford. The middle section between the inclines used Watson 0-4-0 saddle tank engines such as No. 47007, seen at Sheep Pasture stabling point on 5th October 1963, not long before the line was closed.

Below: It has always been seen as unfair that the railway bears the whole cost of its infrastructure, whereas road users perceive their road use as free on entry. On the King's Cross-Aberdeen main line the Forth and Tay bridges in particular give rise to high maintenance costs. This view looking south from Dundee shows the Tay Bridge.

Left: The largest class of main line locomotive on BR numerically was the class 5 4-6-0 by Sir William Stanier. 842 of these useful engines worked all over the former LMS system from as far south as Bournemouth to as far north as Wick. On 21st July 1955 No. 44949 hurries out of Colne in Lancashire with the 11.55am through train to London Euston.

Efficiency

How does one measure the efficiency of a railway? Management text books might pontificate on financial ratios like earnings per share or profit over asset value. Railway passengers (we've only been called customers for the last ten years) might say that low fares, clean trains and good timekeeping are the best measures of efficiency. Freight customers would quote speedy transits and on-time arrivals without damage to their products. Traction engineers would go for

availability, reliability and whole-life costs of their rolling stock. Operators may judge their work by the reduction in overall minutes delay. Governments want to see reductions in the taxpayers' inputs (that is subsidies by all and any names). "Green" bodies want to see much more traffic off the roads.

None of these is inherently wrong, so what did John Major mean when he talked about BR's inefficiency? My guess is that he was referring to the level of subsidy necessary to support BR, compared with the Conservative vision that a privatised railway would need less financial support from the taxpayer (I could say "from the government", but governments have no money of their own - it mostly comes from taxpayers, from you and me and the firms we work for).

None of these measures is actually sufficient on its own. They are interrelated. Each political variation in government has different objectives for the nation's transport system, and also has to take note nowadays of European directives

which may sometimes influence policy significantly.

In this book, I have attempted to judge the actual effects of changes with respect to the effects they were intended to have by the governments of the day, or by the railway management of the period. Underlying all, however, is the total government subsidy needed to keep the railways going. This remains a key issue through much of the 50 years period we are studying.

History of change

The development of the railways of Britain during the last fifty years has added much to railway history. The period has seen the change from private to public, centralised control. There have been various attempts at centralising and then devolving management. Steam traction has been replaced by diesel and electric. Many railway lines and stations have closed. Local authorities have been brought into financing urban railway networks. Many

new stations have opened. Electrification has extended. Early traction has been replaced by much more effective vehicles. Track design has changed from bull-head rail on wooden sleepers maintained by men with spanners and picks and shovels to continuously welded flat-bottomed rail on concrete sleepers maintained by rail-borne machines. Signalling has moved on from mechanical semaphores and relay operated multiple-aspect signals to remotely controlled route setting using progressively more sophisticated forms of electric and electronic control, and to radio-supported operation without signals in remote areas. Computers have taken over most storage and analysis of information from a host of railway clerks. Districts, divisions and regions have all disappeared in recent decades, and have been replaced by "businesses" whose orientation related to the type of service offered. The term "market-led" has gained credence towards the end of an era claimed by some to have formerly seen the railway as "engineering-led".

raditional Edmundson card tickets have
en replacement by various forms of
aper and card tickets, leading to the
opular output of the computerised
ooking offices of the late BR period.
rain liveries and interiors have changed.
arnished teak exteriors and drab paints
ave been thrown out in favour of light
oloured plastic interior finishes, and
orporate, then business, external liveries.
oday's railway is nothing like the one
which BR inherited in 1948. Is it more effi-
ient? Does it meet the government's
bjectives better than did the former
ailway companies? Does it meet its
ustomers' needs better?

eaders of this book will draw their own
onclusions from the situations I discuss
n each chapter.

op Right: Strenuous efforts were made
y BR regions to improve long-distance
ervices. Western Region dominance of
he two routes between London and
xeter resulted in penetration onto the
outhern of WR class 50 Co-Co diesel
lectrics. In 1985, No. 50 046 *Ajax* passes
aynes Park with an afternoon train from
xeter to Waterloo.

eft: Steam locomotives had relatively
hort duty cycles before servicing was
eeded to clean ash pans and fire grates,
nd to take on coal and water. Hundreds
f locomotive depots were located
round the country, several as large as this
ne at Polmadie in south Glasgow. In this
iew, on 10th July 1960, suburban
-6-4Ts and mixed traffic locomotives
redominate.

ight: Later in BR's life, traction utilisation
mproved as trains worked further away
rom their former home areas. At Crewe,
or example, one could see a class 33 Sulzer
o-Bo diesel electric based at Eastleigh
epot working a Manchester to Cardiff
assenger train, adjacent to a class 303
5kV a.c. e.m.u. recently transferred from
he Glasgow area to the Manchester
uburban network, as was seen on 24th
May 1983.

The former railways

Heydays

Before the onset of the second world war the four principal railway companies of Britain were enjoying a period of confident expansion of fast, steam-hauled passenger services at the same time as carrying a huge volume of freight. Around London, the Southern Railway (SR) had electrified its inner suburban routes and its main lines to the central south coast. The London Midland & Scottish Railway (LMS) ran electric suburban trains out of Euston and Broad Street, but otherwise London suburban trains were steam hauled. With the notable exceptions of the Mersey, Wirral, Bury, Altrincham and Tyneside electric lines, other conurbations used steam traction, usually with trains of non-corridor coaches hauled by modern tank engines.

Supporting all this was a vast network of secondary and branch lines. Passenger services on these were generally irregular, often using trains of ancient lineage. The Great Western Railway (GWR), very much a steam railway, broke the mould on a few routes with its neat AEC/Park Royal diesel mechanical railcars. Secondary line freight trains across the country served individual station goods yards and freight handling depots, their engines calling and shunting at many stations during a day-long trip to

Left: The four main pre-war railways in Britain were often praised for their initiatives. On the LMS and LNER in the 1930s, fast travel between Scotland and London was made possible through the scheduling of streamlined trains to specially accelerated timings. Stanier 4-6-2 No. 6220 *Coronation* thunders north through Berkhamsted with the Coronation Scot from Euston to Glasgow. Scenes such as this could not survive the austerity of the war and post-war years. *Maurice W. Earley / National Railway Museum*

Above: The Southern Railway invested heavily in 660V d.c. electrification in the London suburban area and to south coast resorts and commuter towns. To extend early three-car 3-SUB units to four cars, an additional carriage was added, to the wider profile preferred by the SR's chief mechanical engineer, O.V.S. Bulleid. The second vehicle of 4-SUB unit No. 4526 is one of these, seen approaching Clapham Junction, "Britain's busiest railway station". *C.C.B. Herbert / National Railway Museum*

deliver and collect wagons. Once delivered to marshalling yards, individual wagons were shunted onto trains that headed vaguely in the direction of their final destinations, often to endure shunting

at several further marshalling yards on the way. During their journeys they were lost to the outside world: there was no system for tracing a wagon until it turned up at its destination station or yard. Transits were commonly two weeks from loading to unloading. Many took far longer.

The bright stars of the pre-war railways were the streamlined express trains of the LMS and the London & North Eastern Railway (LNER) that linked London with Scotland and the north of England. The Southern Railway was more sedate, but embraced luxury in its group of Pullman trains and boat trains that linked London with the south coast. The LNER also used Pullman trains for its more discerning long distance business passengers. The Great

Western ran one very fast train, the 'Cheltenham Flyer'. Other express services across the country were generally heavy, and their speeds related to what the locomotives could haul rather than what the market needed. Passengers endured train travel, having little alternative in an age when car ownership was the exception rather than the rule. Air travel was for the very rich and the wealthy businessman, although some of the railway companies did own small airlines that later became part of British European Airways. The railway companies owned other ancillary businesses, all related to supporting their travel products. The railway hotels are legendary, and were regarded at the time as models of their

d. Passenger ferries to the continent
d Ireland operated in connection with
at trains. Nearly all civil, signal and train
gineering was carried out in-house, to
e extent that most locomotives and
rriages were designed, built and main-
ned by the railways themselves.
tering was done in-house, not always
ccessfully if the legend of the infamous
ilway sandwich" is to be believed.
ese railways were surviving in commer-
l terms without government subsidy.
ey had relatively captive markets, and
ned enough in profits to enable some
estments to continue. Asset replace-
nt was no longer at a rate necessary to
ep abreast of all renewals, except
rhaps on the SR, but even there the flow
investment cash into electrification gave
e to the retention of many, very old
am locomotives.

Wartime privations

ring the second world war the railway
mpanies were put under central govern-
ent control, at least to ensure they were
equately able to make their physical
ntribution to the war effort. We became
ed to the sight of troop trains seemingly
most anywhere in the country. There
re long trains of war equipment, tanks,
moured vehicles, weapons and ammu-
tion. As these war trains gained in
cendancy, the public were dissuaded
m making rail journeys by slogans such
"Is your journey really necessary?"
ring the war the railways had cash for
eir extended operations, but little
oney for investment or maintenance.
ack maintenance was reduced to that
cessary for a maximum speed of
mph. I remember watching Southern
ilway express trains pass through
eybridge at this speed during the war,
d saw the sleepers bouncing up and
own in the meagre ballast as the trains
ssed over them.
her publications have shown how
uch damage was done by enemy bombs
d shells. Tremendous efforts were
ade to restore traffic around and through
e damaged areas. There are famous

Above: The apparently enormous length of main line freight trains was as much due to the preponderance of relatively small wagons, most of which carried loads of 15 tons or less. Behind the tender of this LMS class 8F 2-8-0 are three cattle wagons and an assortment of open wagons and covered goods vans. The train is heading south on the Midland main line before nationalisation. *Dr. P. Ransome-Wallis / National Railway Museum*

Below: The LMS articulated Beyer Garratt 2-6-0+0-6-2 locomotives worked principally on the Toton (Nottinghamshire) to Brent (London) heavy coal trains that brought household fuel to the capital. This pre-war view shows No. 4994 trundling south through Elstree with a loaded coal train. *H. Gordon Tidey / National Railway Museum*

photographs in archives showing a gaping hole in the St. Pancras station roof, a class A4 Pacific destroyed by a bomb and a huge crater in East Anglia formed by an ammunition train explosion.

By the end of the war the railways and their employees were run down, tired, and worn out. The prospect of restoring peace-time conditions beckoned, but seemed almost unattainable.

Slow recovery

Money was tight after the war as the various participating countries' governments developed ways of paying for the necessary recovery. By 1947 it was clear that the railway companies in Great Britain could not raise enough capital to overtake the enormous backlog of infrastructure and train replacement and maintenance. Moreover, a new political wave of change was moving, following the election of the post-war Labour government. State ownership of the means of production was the theme for progress, and railways were seen as an essential part of the means of production. Thus the policy of nationalisation swept the country. The state took over ownership "by the people" of virtually all the railways including London Transport, much road haulage, several bus companies, docks, canals, airports, electricity generation and distribution, coal mining, gas manufacturing and supply, steel production, aircraft manufacture, road vehicle manufacture, airlines, and airports. In some cases the nation owned the complete industry, in others a major part. On 1st January 1948, the four big railways, the LMS, LNER, GWR and SR, were joined by the Kent & East Sussex Railway, the East Kent Railway, the Mersey Railway and the Cheshire Lines Committee lines to form one, all-embracing body called British Railways. That is where the story in this book really begins. ◄END►

Below: It was not just the LMS, LNER, GWR and SR that were amalgamated to form British Railways on 1st January 1948 Four smaller lines were also brought into the fold, including two of the former Colonel Stephens railways, both in Kent. This 1947 picture of a rural passenger trai shows Kent & East Sussex Railway 0-6-0T No. 3, a second-hand Stroudley class A1X locomotive that had formerly worked on the Southern Railway. *Dr. P. Ransome-Wallis / National Railway Museum*

Above: Another railway that was embraced by nationalisation in 1948 was the Mersey Railway that ran electric services between Birkenhead and Liverpool Central through a double-track tunnel under the River Mersey. This view shows a Mersey Railway train at Birkenhead Central. *National Railway Museum*

Right: The interior of Crewe North signalbox in 1936 shows what was then a modern installation using short levers. The array of block instruments and the large staff complement illustrate how labour-intensive railway working could be. *LMS / National Railway Museum*

The Railway Executive years

Assets and operations

British Railways inherited a network of 19,639 miles of railway route, 8,294 stations, 973 freight marshalling yards, 20,148 locomotives[1] divided into 419 classes[2], 56,425 carriages, and 1,260,185 wagons. There were also 8,793 horses, 43,483 road vehicles and 19,996 containers. Managing, supervising, operating and maintaining this huge system occupied 648,740 staff.

From day one the network was divided up into six regions, the Eastern, North Eastern, London Midland, Western, Southern and

Right: Time- and labour-consuming methods of train working were common in the early years on British Railways. Western Region 43XX class 2-6-0 No. 7317 was collecting a six-wheeled van from the sidings at Marlborough station on Sunday morning 6th January 1957 to attach it to an Andover Junction to Swindon passenger train. The carriages and passengers had to wait in the station for this move to be completed.

Above: Before standard designs of locomotive could be developed by BR, LMS-designed Ivatt 2-6-0s and 2-6-2Ts and Fairburn 2-6-4Ts were chosen to be built for use on other regions. The Southern Region built many LMS-style 2-6-4Ts at its Brighton works, mainly for use in the southeast. Of these, No. 42096 was an unusual visitor to Bournemouth on 11th April 1955 when it was photographed calling at Boscombe with the 3.54pm stopping train from Bournemouth Central to Andover. Passengers at the front of this train still had to put up with carriages built for the former London & South Western Railway before the first world war!

Scottish. Only the Scottish Region merged together routes from two of the former railways; the others basically followed the boundaries of the old railways in England and Wales, the LNER being divided into the ER and NER just north of Doncaster. (BR subsequently made boundary adjust-

ments several times to tidy up penetrating or otherwise illogical areas.)

Fortunately, in any large organisation there is plenty of momentum to keep things running. Unless top management demands immediate changes, people tend to keep on doing things in the same old way. Thus the task of moulding common standards into the fledgling British Railways did not initially get in the way of railway operations which carried on in more or less the same way as before, at least for the first few years. True, there was the early need to make some publicly-visible changes to assert the new regime's existence. The locomotive and rolling stock fleet went through two phases of renumbering, firstly with regional prefixes (e.g. E8619). Later in 1948 the locomotive fleet received newly assigned number ranges that in most cases absorbed the old numbers visibly (e.g. 68619). A range of corporate train liveries was developed using blue for top link express passenger

engines, green for other express engines, lined black for mixed traffic locomotives and plain black for the rest. (The blue was soon eliminated in favour of Brunswick green, on the grounds that the blue pigment faded.) These were to haul red-and-cream corridor coaches (which brightened up the railway scene delightfully) or plain red non-corridor coaches. Freight stock received basically light grey for the stock only fitted with handbrakes and bauxite brown for those with continuous brakes.[3]

Steam continues to rule

The Railway Executive quickly decided that the future would continue to rely largely on steam traction, with development of 1,500V d.c. electrification for longer term development of specific routes. The locomotive exchanges of 1948, in which locomotives of key types

Left: BR's first corporate livery scheme used this attractive light Prussian blue colour for top link express passenger locomotives, as seen in July 1949 on Bulleid 'Merchant Navy' Pacific No. 35017 *Belgian Marine* at Nine Elms depot, London. The blue was later reckoned to lose its colour through pigment failure, and was replaced by the more popular Brunswick green. *Friends of the National Railway Museum / Colour-Rail*

Below Left: BR completed the electrification of the Manchester-Sheffield/Wath route that had been proposed by the LNER before the war. Nearly-new 1,500V d.c. Co-Co electric locomotive No. 27000 passes Dinting with an up Manchester-Sheffield-Marylebone express in 1956. *J.T Inglis / Colour-Rail*

Standard steam

The policy of continuing with steam traction led to the development of twelve new designs of steam locomotive, aimed at replacing the plethora of types inherited from the old railways. While all contained some modern features, only one design met new needs. The two-cylinder class 7 'Britannia' Pacifics, introduced in 1951, had boilers dimensionally similar to the Bulleid 'West Country' class. The 'Britannias' performed outstandingly on the Liverpool Street-Norwich expresses. Their class-mates, the smaller class 6 'Clan' 4-6-2s did adequately on the Glasgow and Carlisle to Stranraer lines, though not so much better than a class 5. The BR class 5 4-6-0 was more of a race-horse than the LMS variety from which it was evolved. Certainly, drivers on the Somerset & Dorset line between Bournemouth and Bath claimed that the BR class 5 boiler could never be beaten - it would always produce more steam than the engine could use however much it was extended. People didn't say that of the class 4 4-6-0s, though later rebuilding with double chimneys went some way to help. The class 4 2-6-4T was a superb design, well-received wherever it was allocated, all over the country from Scotland to Brighton. This can also be said for the

re tested on all regions with namometer cars, enabled different sses to be compared on similar work. comotives and rolling stock to the rmer railways' designs continued to be ilt at least until 1952 as new orders were aced and honoured.

ectrification

r most of this period the railways emed to go on much as before. The ER

electrified out from Liverpool Street to Shenfield, and also completed the LNER's project to wire across the Pennines with electrification of the mainly freight route from Sheffield and Wath to Manchester via Penistone and Woodhead. Both of these schemes used the new standard of 1,500V d.c. with overhead current collection. The SR continued to build "new" suburban electric multiple units by fitting new steel bodies on old underframes and bogies, thus producing large numbers of the 4-SUB and 4-EPB types.

Above: For many years the principal express trains on all regions were entrusted to the class 8P and 7P locomotive classes of the former railways. In March 1954, green 'Merchant Navy' class 4-6-2 No. 35027 *Port Line* prepares to start the Golden Arrow Pullman boat train for Dover Marine out of London's Victoria station. *Stephen Townroe / Colour-Rail*

Below: New building of former railway shunting locomotive typ reached its nadir when the North Eastern Region insisted on repli cating the nineteenth-century class J72 0-6-0Ts for new construction at Darlington works! 1951-built No. 69010 was photographed there after overhaul, in July 1959. *Colour-Rail*

Left: The first batch of new standard locomotives to be built by BR in 1951 was the group of 'Britannia' class 7 Pacifics allocated to the Great Eastern section of the Eastern Region. These revolutionised performance on the Liverpool Street to Norwich expresses, enabling a regular two-hour timing to be operated. On 1st November 1958, 70008 *Black Prince* was receiving concentrated attention from cleaners at Stratford depot.

Below Left: The free-steaming BR standard class 5 4-6-0 type was inevitably compared with the LMS class 5 design, sometimes unfavourably because of the BR engines' harder ride. No. 73061 drifts down Grayrigg bank on the Carlisle to Preston section with a mixed freight early on 7th July 1962.

intervals of around 90,000 miles, well above the 60,000 or so achieved by most regional types. (Even so, when a BR class 4 2-6-4T was stripped in Eastleigh works during my apprenticeship, fitters remarked that there were almost twice as many small parts in the component trays than a 'King Arthur' 4-6-0 would have released!) The advent of the BR engines allowed scrapping of many of the multitude of ancient and old-fashioned engines of pre-grouping (i.e. pre-1923) origin. Later ones enabled early "big four" railway types to be withdrawn as well.

While former LMS travellers probably found the new BR mark 1 main line corridor coaches an improvement on what they had formerly been used to, there was puzzlement on the SR, WR (to a lesser extent), the ER/NER and parts of the Scottish Region as to why the new coaches were so noisy and dimly lit.

No real change

During all this time, the main line diesels 10000 and 10001 and the SR trio 10201 to 10203 worked on the LMR and then the SR, gaining high mileages by combining steam operating diagrams. The success of

...her smaller BR standard designs, the ...6-0s and the 2-6-2Ts, though something ...t quite right with the steaming of the ...ass 2 2-6-0 had to be attended to by the ...cellent team of engineers at Swindon. ...e one design that met a long-felt new ...ed was the 9F 2-10-0. Brilliant ...rformers, the 2-10-0s took over heavy ...ights, enabling the LMS Beyer Garratt ...ticulated engines to be scrapped, and

speeded up other freight flows or enabled loads to be increased. More 9Fs were built than any other BR standard type, to a total of 221 locomotives.

Probably the greatest contribution to efficiency that the BR standard engines made was their extended periods between works overhaul. The use of manganese steel horn guides and axlebox liners enabled lifting of the larger locomotives to be extended to

Right: There were antiquities all over B
Because of the uniqueness of the Isle of
Wight railways' loading gauge, particularl
the tunnel at Ryde, small locomotives and
short carriages from pre-1923 railways w
used there right up to the late 1960s. Aft
arrival from Ryde Pier Head on 24th June
1956, class O2 0-4-4T No. W18 *Ningwoo*
pauses at Ventnor for removal of ash from
the smoke box, a chore that was needed
every return trip.

Left: Only the Southern Region had
extensive electrification, inherited from it
pre-war investment spree. On 28th May
1960, 4-SUB unit No. 4695, formed of
Bulleid-style steel bodies on much older
underframes and bogies, comes off the
flyover approaching Norwood Junction.
During the early years on BR, policy for
extension of electrification was for more
750V d.c. third rail on the SR, and 1,500V
d.c. overhead electrification elsewhere.

carriers" - they could not turn away traffi
however unprofitable or inconvenient it
would be to carry. Yes, there were some
better locomotives, but they were doing
the same work in the same way as their
forebears. Passenger traffic would soon
bleeding slowly away to the new family
cars (remember the Austin A35, the Mor
Minor and the early Ford Anglia**?**). Freig
consists were still being delayed and
mislaid on the network as they were
shunted from train to train and yard to
yard. A lot of goods traffic was soon to b
lost to the burgeoning road haulage
industry. Realisation of what to do abou
these things did not dawn for a long time
At this stage, the British Transport
Commission (BTC), to whom the Railwa
Executive (RE) was responsible, had a
huge portfolio of diverse nationalised
transportation to oversee. Its accounts d
not readily reveal where within the railways money was being made and where
was being lost. It was not possible to
monitor which regions were being well
managed and which, if any, were not.
Neither was it possible to show readily
which railway routes made a surplus and
which did not. ▄▄END▄▄

American diesel locomotives in the USA,
Canada and around the world was noted
by many engineers. The Railway
Executive appeared unable, however, to
come off their policy of relying on steam
locomotives until widespread electrification could be afforded. They had set up a
system of management through functional
departments, regionally based but guided
strongly from the centre. Policy was
centralised. The regions would run the
railway, the central executive would set

standards and decide on the way forward.
One can only afford investment if there is
cash coming in through profits. British
Railways was not very profitable, and
was heading for its period of sustained
losses. There was no money to pay for
extensive electrification.

The railways were not potentially profitable because all the old inefficiencies of
the former railways were still there, and
tariffs were being held low by government
decree. Railways were still "common

Power to the regions

De-centralisation

With such centralisation of control that the Railway Executive had taken unto itself, it was little wonder that day-to-day management of the changes that were needed in order to respond to evolving market conditions was difficult. A classic remedy for making an unwieldy organisation more manageable is to devolve some of the key decision-making to the next level down in the structure. Thus it was in the mid-1950s that the chief regional officers, as they had been known, found themselves with greater powers within their own regions. In recognition of this change they became regional general managers, a title that lasted almost unscathed through the next four decades.

Dissatisfied with the financial situation of the railways, the BTC had taken steps to grasp closer policy control of what was happening on the railways. They dismantled the Railway Executive and placed more responsibility into the hands of the general managers of the regions.

Right: The new regime introduced by the British Transport Commission in 1956 gave regions much more autonomy in their actions. The Eastern Region painted up the Liverpool Street station pilot locomotive, class J69 0-6-0T No. 68619, in the pre-1923 dark blue livery of the former Great Eastern Railway and kept it specially clean for this duty.

Above: The London Midland Region was early in building new, light-weight diesel multiple units in its works at Derby. Other units were purchased from Metro-Cammell in Birmingham. The new trains were employed initially in west Yorkshire, Cumbria and on lightly used lines in East Anglia. This two-car Derby set was photographed at Stratford depot, east London, on 11th May 1957.

This enabled the regions to show their different management characteristics. Some were able to move forward to grasp the opportunities ahead. Some embraced modernisation positively. They were usually the same regions that were willing to grasp the nettle and close, quietly and with minimal political fuss, railway routes, goods yards and stations that

clearly generated insufficient traffic or which duplicated others. Thus the ER and WR (at least) began the process of line closures that was inevitable if the loss-makers were to be removed. During this period the former Midland & Great Northern route that linked the east coast main line with the Norfolk coast closed, as did most of the Didcot, Newbury & Southampton line, the Midland & Great Western route that crossed the south west of England from Andover Junction to Cheltenham, and the wild track over Stainmore summit between Penrith/Tebay and Barnard Castle. Meanwhile, the LMR took part in the first serious attempt at modernising the rolling stock fleet. A fleet of two-car diesel hydraulic, lightweight railcars was brought into use, built in the LMR's Derby works. Each car was powered, and the

resultant good acceleration, matched by quick-action two-pipe vacuum brake, enabled faster timings to be introduced o stopping trains between Leeds and Bradford. These were introduced in 195 and raised traffic substantially, thus pointing the way for later schemes. The LMR also put diesel railcars and trailers into service in the rural Cumbrian distric late in 1954, this time with the mechanic transmission that became the BR standar for four decades.

The BTC meanwhile was grappling with the enormous task of trying to manage docks, harbours, canals, road services, bu services, London Transport and the six railway regions, without a body in place pull the management of BR together. It was clearly too much. Losses were begin ning to become serious, and solutions needed to be found.

bove: A visible sign of the devolved gime was the decision to change ssenger carriage liveries from red-and-eam (or the all-over red of non-corridor aches) to a near copy of the former LMS aroon. The SR opted for a darker shade of een than its former Malachite, and the WR ent for brown-and-cream on its principal xpresses. With maroon BR mark 1 stock in w, class A4 4-6-2 No. 60020 *Guillemot* ces past Hatfield on 15th April 1960 with e 11am from King's Cross to Edinburgh.

he apparent success of the West Riding esel scheme, the reliance being placed in me other countries on modern (i.e. non-eam) forms of traction, the depressing ate of most railway stations and the palling working conditions of the ilway staff who worked day in and day t with steam locomotives were leading ilway and public opinion to demand odernisation of the railways.

Below: To speed up the reduction of costs, most regions made efforts to close those railway routes that had high losses. The former Didcot, Newbury & Southampton Railway route ran its last passenger trains on 5th March 1960. Gracing the footplate of Collett 0-6-0 No. 2240 at Winchester Chesil on the last northbound train, the 5.12pm from Eastleigh to Didcot, is Eastleigh district motive power superintendent Stephen Townroe, solemnly attired for the occasion.

Modernisation

The need

Hindsight makes writers seem wiser than we are! As a railway enthusiast and a young railway engineer, I admit to having been comfortable with the Railway Executive's steam traction policy. I suppressed what misgivings I might have had over the apparent reluctance to embrace more modern traction. Looking back, we can see how wrong the RE's approach had been. There were diesel and electric locomotive manufacturers in this country who would have been delighted to have their products running on the home railways so that they could demonstrate them to potential overseas customers. How the English Electric Company managed to convince so many railways abroad to buy its main line diesel locomotives when only five were working at home is one of the wonders of this period! But for BR to have purchased large numbers of diesels in the early 1950s would have cost so much that fewer would have been afforded, so that less progress could have been made in the elimination of steam locomotives. Similar cost arguments would have been made about the policy to extend 1,500V d.c. electrification. BR simply did not have

Right: Despite modernisation of BR's trains, track, signalling and some stations, train working otherwise remained as before, with new locomotives being used on out-dated yard transfer workings such as this one leaving Hither Green in London on 20th May 1960 behind brand new BRCW/Sulzer diesel electric Bo-Bo Type 3 No. D6553. The train was marshalled with brake vans at each end to facilitate direction reversals during its cross-London working. Note the new multiple-aspect signal gantry almost ready for use and which was presumably about to replace the semaphore on the left.

Above: Heavy for their task, the Type 2 A1A-A1A diesel electric design by Brush initially used Mirrlees diesel engines that produced 1,250hp. No. D5802 was photographed leaving Cambridge with the 10.36am from Liverpool Street to King's Lynn on 7th August 1961. The Mirrlees engines were subsequently replaced by English Electric 1,470hp units.

Top Right: The 25kV a.c. electrification between Crewe and Manchester/Liverpool brought to BR five designs of similar-looking locomotives, all with different mechanical and electrical equipment. Resplendent in its new 'electric blue' livery, an English Electric Type A (passenger) locomotive, No. E3029, poses at the newly modernised Manchester Piccadilly station (formerly London Road) before departure on 10th July 1961 with the Pines Express for Bournemouth.

Bottom Right: Two Western Region diesel hydraulic B-Bs from the lower-powered Type 2 group produced by North British (NBL), Nos. D6305 and D6303, enter Lostwithiel station in Cornwall on 23rd July 1960 with a down summer Saturday express. There are no other signs of modernisation in this picture which shows typical GWR railway fixed equipment.

enough money to do it. Remember that in those days, all railway losses and investment had to be met by borrowing. As I have stated before in this book, the BTC accounts did not readily indicate all the areas in which the money was being lost. Managers had to use their eyes, ears, intuition and common sense to judge where the greatest inefficiencies were. Steam traction became the scape-goat.

A new vision

The 1955 modernisation plan was supported by the Conservative government with hard cash, £1,240 million to be spent over 15 years. I remember politicians

saying, "It's not whether we can afford the plan, it's whether we can afford not to do it!", thus setting the public's mind on the matter of the taxpayer footing the bill. Steam would be eliminated progressively by dieselisation and electrification. The west coast main line between London, Birmingham, Manchester and Liverpool, the former Great Eastern and LT&S suburban services around north-east London, and local services around Glasgow would be electrified using the bold, new 25kV 50cycles/second a.c. system that the French had made successful on the Valenciennes-Thionville scheme, but modified to 6.25kV in areas of tight electrical clearances. The SR third rail d.c. network would be extended to the

Kent main lines and progressively upgraded to 750V. All other traction replacement would be by diesel locomotives or diesel multiple units purchased from British manufacturers.

The plan also moved towards extension the use of flat-bottomed rails on concret sleepers for main lines (later to be improved with continuously welded rails), the reduction of mechanical semaphore signalling on main lines, and improvements to the very worst main li stations. New freight marshalling yards were built at Temple Mills in east Londo Margam in South Wales, Tyne near Newcastle, Tinsley and Toton in the Midlands, Mossend near Glasgow, Thornton in Fife and Thornaby in the north-east. The railway route through Tonbridge, Reading, Oxford and Bletchl was designated a round-London trunk route. The prominent, concrete Bletchle flyover was built to separate slow movin freight flows at the junction with the we coast main line. (In practice, little freight was diverted to use the route as the volume of freight began to plummet.)

New traction and rolling stock

Electric locomotives built for the west coast scheme were proposed to one bas layout, a mixed-traffic, 3,300hp, double cab Bo-Bo equipped with one transformer and mercury-arc rectifier to convert the a.c. current to d.c. for the fo traction motors. Five British manufacturers produced different designs of locomotives to this specification[4]. All b a handful were geared for 100mph oper tion, the exceptions being geared for 80mph top speed and designated as freight locomotives. They worked well despite what in retrospect seems the unlikely success of mobile mercury arc rectification. In time, solid state power electronics were deemed sufficiently robust to replace the arc rectifiers. Electric multiple units were generally based on BR standard carriage designs using BR single bolster or Gresley bogie

Above: Despite their relatively slow acceleration, the ER introduced Cravens lightweight diesel multiple units on the King's Cross inner-suburban services. Type 2 locomotives worked the outer service. Two Cravens twin sets approach Potter's Bar 15th April 1960 on a Welwyn Garden City to Finsbury Park working.

The exception was in Scotland where a more modern body style was adopted employing power operated sliding doors for passenger access.

In common with most diesel multiple units, the Scottish electric trains had a clear forward view for passengers sitting in the saloon behind the driver, a very popular feature at the time. All the electric train purchases provided a step change of performance improvement over the trains they replaced.

The policy for diesel traction was, as with the electric locomotives, to buy from several suppliers. In this case, because Britain's experience with diesel traction was perceived to be so limited, BR placed orders with as many manufacturers as were willing to supply diesel locomotives in pilot groups of ten or twenty examples. This included some of BR's own workshops. The idea was to evaluate the pilot locomotives in service before choosing standard types for large scale purchase. Diesel electrics were to be the norm, divided into four 'type' groups based on power output, Type 1 being the lowest (1,000hp and below) and Type 4 the

highest (above 2,000hp). With the Type 4s limited to 90mph top speed, there was not much performance improvement when the diesels were compared with the steam locomotives they replaced, except in those areas where smaller steam types were replaced by larger diesels such as on the Midland main line.

The diesel multiple units were generally based on the popular type that Derby works delivered to the Cumbrian lines in 1954, but with improvements. Heavier vehicles with all-steel bodies were included in the orders, large quantities of which went to all carriage builders interested in supplying. In this case prototypes were deemed to be unnecessary in view of the experience already built up.

Two regions were able to convince the mechanical and electrical engineer's department that they could adopt non-standard diesel traction. The WR ordered

diesel hydraulic locomotives from Swindon works and from North British Glasgow. The SR decided on diesel electric multiple units that would have components standard with their latest electric multiple units.

As the potential of diesel locomotives became more widely appreciated operators and politicians began to demand a speeding up of the replacement of steam traction. Almost as soon as the first deliveries of pilot diesel locomotives were being received by BR in 1957 came political pressure to order large quantities to ensure the total elimination of steam traction at the earliest opportunity. Yet the speed at which it all had to happen meant that there was no time to select a favoured design out of the pilot groups within each power range. It was necessary to order from all but one of the chosen manufacturers at once and to receive and

mission their dissimilar products into
vice in parallel.

e arrival of so many new diesel locomo-
es on all the regions of BR tested
erely the ability of each region to
bond. Most regions retrained staff who
l been brought up on steam, using as
ners such young and adaptable engi-
rs they had who could master the new
chines quickly. The operators had a
e task in training drivers, particularly in
face of the railway unions' stand that
most senior drivers should benefit
m the new traction first. Thus those
o were inherently the least adaptable,
oldest drivers, had to master the new
ction in a short time, led by people who
mselves were just learning. I stand
azed that it worked as well as it did.

action developments

ond the second wave of diesel deliv-
es, there was scope for experience to
erge, and for designs that bore the fruit
hat experience to be produced. Thus,
er the very heavy 1Co-Co1 designs of
pe 4s, came the Brush Type 4 Co-Cos, of
ich 532 were eventually provided, the
gest class of main line diesel locomotive
merically to run in Britain. The Brush
pe 4s were probably the operators' most
eful locomotive class ever, capable of
ling 95mph passenger expresses and
00 ton oil trains with apparently equal
e. At about the same time, English
ctric produced their excellent Type 3
-Co design, another class that became a
st reliable work horse. On the Western
gion, diesel hydraulic development
oduced the useful 1,700hp B-B Hymek
pe 3 locomotives and the more
werful, 2700hp, 100mph Western class
C-Cs, both of which were produced in
atively large numbers. Of the 650hp 0-
diesel hydraulic freight transfer
comotives that Swindon produced, for
ich the market appeared to collapse
ernight, the least said the better.
ually, the centre-cab Clayton Bo-Bo
pe 1 diesel electrics that appeared in
lume for the Scottish and North Eastern
gions soon lost their usefulness as coal

Top: A major development of the later stages of the modernisation programme was the introduction of the 22 Deltic Co-Co diesel electrics to replace 55 Pacific steam locomotives. BR's first 100mph diesels brought new standards of performance to the east coast main line, to such famous trains as the Flying Scotsman, seen here approaching Finsbury Park southbound on 5th August 1961 behind the first of the class, No. D9000, then unnamed.

Above: For very lightly used branch lines some hope of survival was offered by the purchase of two-axle diesel mechanical railbuses, similar to Germany's Uerdingen cars. Several firms built small batches, one being A.C. Cars whose railbus No. 79976 was at Swindon on new year's day 1961. They were not comfortable-riding vehicles, and the losses on their routes were too great to prevent ultimate closure. Their lives on BR were little more than ten years.

Above: New station buildings were promised, though very few actually transpired. Banbury's replacement buildings still stand today (1998).

Right: NBL built diesel electric Bo-Bo Type 2s, initially for the Eastern and Scottish Regions, though all of them quickly gravitated north of the border. D6142 brings a south-bound freight off the Forth Bridge at Dalmeny on 14th July 1960.

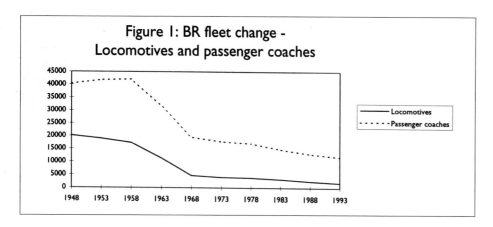

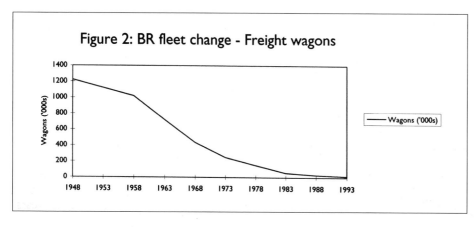

and general freight declined, and they al had relatively short lives.

The most non-standard class was the Deltic Co-Co design introduced in 196 This was the result of the east coast regions joining forces together and demanding something that could utter and completely beat steam performanc on a railway where steam had performe well. Over 3,000hp was needed with a maximum speed of 100mph. English Electric's prototype Deltic had been trie and proved competent. 22 Deltics were purchased with the aim of replacing 55 Pacific steam locomotives. The Deltics were technically delicate machines and first needed much engineering nursing. Nonetheless they became the nation's favourite fast diesel locomotives, and as side effect brought otherwise steam-oriented railway enthusiasts around to appreciate the value of some types of modern traction.

Another innovation that appeared in the modernisation plan period was the grou of self-contained, diesel electric Pullma trains built for the Manchester-St. Pancr route on the LMR and the Bristol and Birmingham main lines on the WR. The were the first air-conditioned trains that ever travelled in, and were distinctive in their modern and comfortable appoint-ment. They maintained fast timings aim at the business markets.

As the effects of modernisation becam clear, people began to ask: was the railway moving into profit? The answe was a definitive "No!". The decline int loss-making continued. The railways' borrowings to meet losses were on the up and up, shattering the politicians' dream that modernisation would bring the railways into profit. The reasons were still not clear, being subsumed in the complicated accounts of the British Transport Commission. **END**

The Beeching era

Appointment from industry

By 1960 it was evident that the route for British Railways to move from a loss making entity to a profit making one had not been established. The Conservative government now had the dynamic figure of Ernest Marples as minister of transport. He set about acquiring from British industry a man expected to be able to create and deliver an incisive analysis of the situation facing British Railways in such a way that the system could be turned round financially and brought into profit within a few years. Dr. Richard Beeching came from Imperial Chemical Industries (ICI), initially as a part time member of the British Transport Commission as the first step to taking over the BTC chair when General Sir Brian Robertson retired on 1st June 1961. Organisationally, the government was determined to dismantle the huge and relatively unresponsive BTC, giving each nationalised transport undertaking its own board with some autonomy over its activities, subject to ministerial overview of key issues. As a result, the British Railways Board (BRB) was set up, legally from 1st January 1963, and was able to give a lead on policy over what were to be turbulent years that followed[5].

Studies, and the Beeching report

A great deal of information emerged from the studies that Dr. Beeching carried through. The report *The Reshaping of British Railways*[6] which was published by the [BRB] in 1963 showed that, by analysis of the 1961 accounts and of other statistics:

gross receipts were £475 million; working expenses were £562 million; th[us] there was a working deficit of £87 milli[on] when interest charges were added, the total deficit was £136 million;

out of the £562 million working expen[ses] the provision, maintenance, stabling an[d] servicing of traction and rolling stock accounted for £157 million or 28%; trai[n] operations including marshalling and shunting accounted for £142 million or 25%; track and signalling together only accounted for £111 million or 20%; ter[mi]nals, cartage and road delivery cost £77 million or 15%; and documentation, claims, and administration came to £65 million or 12%;

only types of traffic that were prof-
ble (i.e. that covered their direct and
irect costs) were, surprisingly, freight
coaching train which was mainly
cels and mails (£7 million surplus) and
l (£3 million surplus). Of the rest, the
ly traffics to earn enough revenue to
er their direct costs were fast and semi-
passenger trains (£19 million cover)
d minerals (£8 million);

big loss-makers were stopping
ssenger trains (revenue £26 million
der direct costs), wagonload freight (£32
llion under) and sundries, that is small
ds of which several made up a
gonload (£14 million under direct
sts);

ypical steam hauled train on a low-
ffic single track railway cost about 15
llings a mile to run; a diesel multiple
t on the same service cost between 4
d 6 shillings a mile;

en if passenger train fares were halved,
ffic would have to rise four-fold just to
er the direct costs of a stopping
vice;

alysis of freight movements between
rious locations such as road to station,
ck to siding and siding to siding
owed that all of them lost money except
ling to siding traffic;

the 946,998 wagons with which BR
rted the year 1961, the average wagon
de 26 loaded journeys in the year, that
one loaded journey every two weeks;
started 1948 with 648,740 staff. By
62 this has come down to 474,538, a
duction of 27%, or 2.2% per year.

e report made fifteen recommendations,
m which I extract these key proposals:

scontinuance of many stopping
ssenger services and closure of a high
oportion of small stations to
ssenger traffic;

lective improvement of inter-city
ssenger services and rationalisation
routes;

mping down of seasonal peaks and
nsequential withdrawal of
ssenger stock;

-ordination of suburban train and bus
vices and charges, in collaboration with

Top: With concentration of all London-Manchester passenger traffic on to the former L&NWR route, fifteen miles of the Midland main line from St. Pancras to Manchester were closed in Derbyshire. This deprived the Midlands cities of Leicester, Nottingham and Derby of a direct service to Manchester. 4F 0-6-0 No. 43935 approaches Miller's Dale in the Peak District in 1963 with a stopping train from Derby to Manchester Central.

Above: Even though the freight route from Par to Fowey survived for china clay traffic, there was under Dr. Beeching's criteria no case for the passenger service from Lostwithiel to the port. Ex-GWR 0-4-2T No. 1419 arrives at Fowey with a two-coach auto-train on 6th June 1960.

Left: The general public think no more of the Beeching era than that it was a period in which up to a third of BR's route mileage was shut down; many main lines that offered alternative routings between major cities were closed. One of these was the former Great Central route from Sheffield Victoria to London Marylebone where class V2 2-6-2 No. 60854 arrived with the up Master Cutler train on 28th September 1957.

municipal authorities, with the alternative of fares increases and possible railway closures;

increase of block train movement of coal (this led to the "merry-go-round" concept for power station coal, and to coal concentration depots for household coal);

concentration on more siding-to-siding traffic and closure of small freight stations;

development of "liner trains", that is container trains (this led to the establishment of the Freightliner network);

concentration of freight sundries on no more than 100 main depots, and linking them with liner trains for movement;

continuation of the drive to eliminate steam traction and withdrawal of carriages and wagons made surplus by the other recommendations;

rationalisation of the road cartage fleet.

Note that at least six recommendations included positive elements and were not totally negative as is generally thought of the reshaping report.

Above: This northbound returning enthusiast special on the Somerset & Dorset section the Southern Region was run in 1963 because the end of the railway was believed to be imminent. The locomotive is 7F 2-8-0 No. 53808, and the location near Corfe Mullen. A major alternative route for south coast to north of England trains existed via Reading and Oxford. Although the closure was heavily contested, the S&D line did finally shut in 1966

Top Right: The short branch in Scotland from Connel Ferry to Ballachulish failed to earn enough revenue to survive. On 11th July 1960, former Caledonian Railway 0-4-4T No. 55238 awaited departure from the outer terminus with the branch train.

Bottom Right: An anachronism was the electric tramway between Grimsby and Immingham that had been operated by a main line railway since GCR days. In this view, former GCR car No. 4 approaches the reversal point at Immingham Town on 18th October 1960. The closures of the tramway and of adjacent branch railway services left Immingham without direct passenger rail access, even though a busy freight railway continues to operate from it to this day.

Closures

Part 2 of the report included the famous maps that illustrated the BRB's view of the railway routes that should be put up for closure. During the period in which the studies were being done, Mr. Marples had called a halt to the line closures that the regions had been progressing. This mora-torium lasted for about one year. The lis of potential line closures in the report resulted from an analysis of the traffic by value carried on each route. Because of t almost total lack of meaningful geograph ical detail in the financial accounts withir BR, the analysis had to be based on

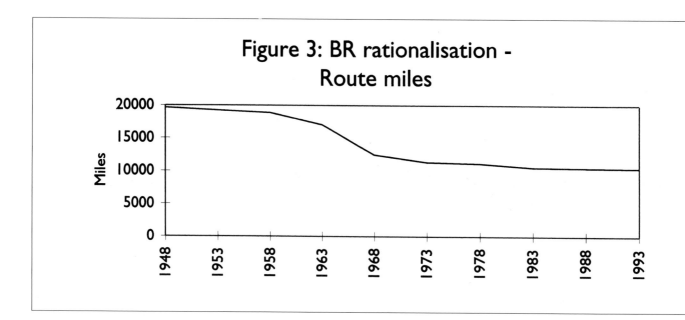

Figure 3: BR rationalisation - Route miles

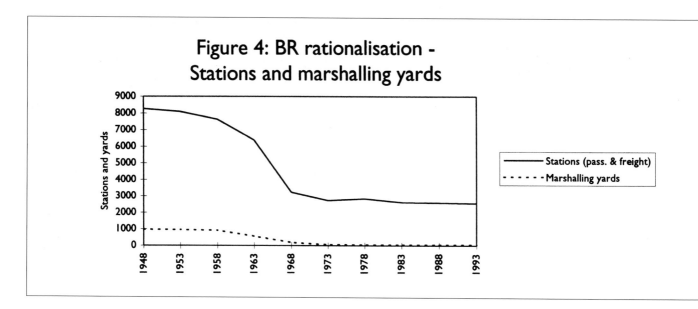

Figure 4: BR rationalisation - Stations and marshalling yards

Stations (pass. & freight)
Marshalling yards

average costs of different types of routes and traffic, and by nature was therefore at times crude. The resulting lists of railway lines and stations for closure would require consultation through the usual channels, including the Transport Users' Consultative Committees whose remit was to highlight potential hardship arising from railway line closures.

The government accepted the report, and the BRB proceeded rapidly to promulgate batches of closure notices. Regional managements undertook the delicate task of consulting their staff on the details of the changes, including the methods by

which people would be dealt with: these were times of virtually full national employment, and many chose to leave for other industries; others were able to be placed in other jobs on BR; yet others were able to take redundancy. That the changes were implemented without serious or prolonged industrial action speaks volumes for the careful preparation by the Board and management of the details of the processes.

True, there were vociferous protests from all around the country. Politicians who had supported the idea of turning the railways round financially were less happy

when their own constituents' jobs were threatened or when the railway line in their own "back yard" was to be closed. Over the next four years or so over 80% of the proposed closures did actually take place. (The maps at the beginning and end of this book contrast the density of the BR network in 1948 and 1994, the last year of BR ownership of the infrastructure.[7])

The election of a Labour government in the middle of the process, however, changed the procedures somewhat. Line closures then had to be referred to the minister of transport, and then later also to the new Regional Economic Planning

Above: Towns and cities with more than one main railway station such as Gloucester were targeted for economies. As a relief to the northbound Pines Express enters Eastgate station on Saturday 30th August 1958, class 5 4-6-0 No.44659 awaits departure with a summer Saturday holiday special from the north of England to the south coast, while 4F 0-6-0 No. 44203 stands at the head of a stopping train for the Midland route, possibly to Bristol. Gloucester's Eastgate station was eventually closed in favour of Central.

Results

...owing what Dr. Beeching achieved, it ...ill come as no surprise to see that the BR ...orking deficit, which had been £87 ...illion in 1961 and which had risen to ...04 million in 1962, began to drop in ...963. The 1963 and 1964 figures were £82 ...d £68 millions respectively. Then, rises

in key costs began to push them up again. True, the railway had been released from some of the restraints caused by being a common carrier, and from the effects of governments refusing raises in passenger fares to the levels asked for by BR, but changes resulting from these would take some time to work through into the final

results. There had been a review in 1960 by a Conservative government-inspired team (the Guillebaud report was the outcome) of the levels of railway staff wages and salaries compared with other industries. The review reached the inevitable and correct conclusion that railway remuneration was far below that

...ards and Councils. This took the steam ...t of the last batches of closures, putting ...lays into the process, and enabled some ...utes actually to escape closure.

paid elsewhere. That was one reason for the relative inability of BR to recruit high quality people. Another was the difficult working conditions, which only the complete demise of steam traction would better. Thus during the Beeching era quite sizeable wage increases were given to railwaymen, well ahead of improvements in individual or corporate productivity. At about this time there was also the slowing down of action on closures following intervention by the new Labour government. These changes cumulatively caused the working deficit (that is before interest charges) to increase again, to £73 million in 1965, virtually nullifying the effects of rationalising and improving the railway.

The trunk route report

In 1965 the BRB published Dr. Beeching's second major report, on the future of the railway trunk routes[8]. By the time of its appearance there was already much aggravation around the country about the effects of the reshaping programme. It was probably not the time to present yet more maps to the public and their politicians! The maps showed the routes that were selected for development, a more positive term that the negative one of listing those for relegation to a lower category or even for closure. But inevitably people read into the maps the idea that main lines such as those between Newcastle and Edinburgh, Leeds and Carlisle, Southampton and Weymouth, west of Plymouth, the Berks and Hants,

and many others were being placed at risk of closure. Politicians were not ready for yet another fundamental uproar.

Leaving

Dr. Beeching left BR in 1965, earlier than the full five year term of his contract. He left in place on BR the liner trains and Inter-City, merry-go-round coal trains, new staff appraisal and training schemes, management training with a business focus, work study, understandable financial controls, a modern corporate identity programme and good plans for the future that might have brought BR into profit again if the politicians had allowed.

Above: Dr. Beeching was able to leave the chairmanship of BR knowing that he had contributed a great deal that was positive in the management philosophy of the railway, including a much more professional awareness of how to identify and manage costs, major strides in developing management training, the application of work measurement and the introduction of new types of bulk freight trains. *Lady Beeching collection*

Top Left: The 20,000-plus road cartage vehicles were reckoned to be a very expensive method of handling freight deliveries even though rail undertook the trunk haul. Siding-to-siding rail traffic was to be preferred economically, such as was epitomised by the new "merry-go-round" coal trains and liner trains that Dr. Beeching's era produced. Scenes such as in this photograph soon became part of railway history. *National Railway Museum*

Bottom Left: Moving less-than-wagonload goods in large containers on dedicated fixed-formation trains of flat wagons was seen to be the most promising way to maximise railway productivity in the general goods sector. Large, articulated lorries did the road collection and delivery function, with the eventual aim of farming this out to private road operators. Relatively few Freightliner depots were required to give reasonable coverage of the country. This view in 1976 shows a large Arrol gantry crane transferring a loaded open container at the Gushetfaulds depot in Glasgow.

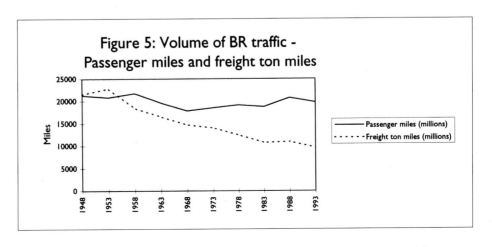

Figure 5: Volume of BR traffic - Passenger miles and freight ton miles

BR Workshops

Inheritance

At the times in the life of a locomotive, carriage or wagon when the mechanical parts could turn, slide or oscillate no more without risk of doing damage, or the boilers could be steamed no more without risk of leaking or cracking, or the varnish and paintwork were no longer considered acceptable, a visit to one of the main workshops for overhaul was required. By 1962 there were still 28 of these large factories, a dating back to the many pre-grouping railways (i.e. pre-1923). Some of these works specialised in dealing with locomotives, others overhauled carriages, and still other repaired freight wagons. A few were

Left: Probably the most famous erecting shop of them all, Swindon's 'A' shop was laid out spaciously around traversers which gave direct access to each locomotive bay. On 1st January 1956, Western Region 'County' class 4-6-0 No. 1017 *County of Hereford* was awaiting completion of an overhaul that had included a complete repaint. Swindon was one of the main works that were listed in the 1962 workshops plan for continued operation, with investment in facilities to take it into the modern traction era.

Workshops plan

In 1962 the BRB published its Workshops Plan. Under the chairmanship of industrialist Sir Steuart Mitchell, a far-reaching plan of rationalisation was proposed, but with heavy investment in the twelve works that were deemed required for the future overhaul of the new railway's traction and rolling stock. The plan unfolded over several years as steam overhauls reduced and space within the longer-term works could be cleared for refurbishment. I was fortunate to be involved in a junior way in different stages of the process. In 1963 to 1965 I was based in the BR Workshops headquarters at Derby, charged with balancing the overhaul workload between the different locomotive works. Thus I monitored the transfer of overhauls of steam locomotives between works, including the movement of many former LMS design locomotives for overhaul at Darlington and Eastleigh. Again, when posted as repairs engineer at Eastleigh, I was able to contribute to the effort to build and operate a progressive carriage repair layout right in the middle of the former locomotive works, when carriage repairs were transferred there from the much larger, adjacent carriage works prior to the latter's closure in 1967. And that was only a very few years after Eastleigh carriage works had absorbed the coaching stock overhaul work from the closure of Lancing works.

No necessary expense was spared in providing the revitalised workshops with the space, tools and equipment to undertake their future tasks. Modern management methods were employed to

ompetent to handle two of these groups, ut very few indeed could manage all three. n particular, the locomotive works had pent all their lives overhauling and epairing steam locomotives. The new eet of diesel and electric locomotives as only just beginning to require any orm of serious works attention.

Experience of diesels and electrics was limited to those works that had been entrusted with their construction. The rapid reduction in the size of the steam locomotive fleet, and the greater specialisation required to cope with the new types of power, suggested that radical changes were required in the railway workshops.

Left: Stratford locomotive works in east London was destined for closure in the workshops plan, but its facilities survived in the form of a heavy repair depot for the Eastern Region. In its former days as a main works, Stratford erecting shop was giving mechanical attention on 7th July 1956 to two ER Thompson locomotives, class L1 2-6-4T No. 67740 and B1 4-6-0 No. 61052 *Brian Morrison*

Below Left: Of the former Southern Region works, Ashford and Lancing were closed and Eastleigh's carriage works was transferred into the middle of the locomotive works site. Eastleigh locomotive work had already embraced diesel power units, as seen in this view of 4SRKT units from diesel electric multiple units being overhauled there.

improve productivity. The use of critical path analysis for planning and managing overhaul work at all the main works led to a massive reduction in the time taken to overhaul locomotives and carriages. In turn that led to a significant reduction in the number of vehicles stopped for overhaul. During my time at Eastleigh, we managed to reduce the time to overhaul and test a Sulzer Type 3 on intermediate overhaul from five weeks to three. We also reduced the number of carriages at the works from over 300 in 1967 to 110 in 1968 with output being slightly up.

I include this short piece on the workshop as an illustration of what was happening all over BR. New ideas, rationalisation, improved methods, investment in the future - it was not just a time of negative retrenchment as some commentators would suggest.

Later, when steam had gone completely, more works had to close. Then, as experience of running the new forms of traction gave rise to new designs that could run twice as far between overhauls, there was yet more rationalisation. The BR Workshops division was eventually to become British Rail Engineering Limited, but that is part of a much later story. ■

Right: The new 1967 layout for over-hauling carriages of all types at the combined Eastleigh works was based on the progressive principle in which each vehicle moved from stage to stage as its work progressed. Vehicle downtimes in this layout were among the lowest at any works within BR Workshops Division. Carriage body stripping and repairs were able to be done in parallel with attention to underframes and bogies, thus saving time. SR Portsmouth express and BR Hastings units are seen receiving C1 and C3 overhauls. *British Rail*

Below: Some of the large redundant works sites like Eastleigh carriage works and Caerphilly locomotive works became private industrial estates. Brighton works had been closed by the Southern Region before the onset of the BR workshops plan. Stroudley class A1X 0-6-0T No. 32646 was shunting the almost empty yard at Brighton on 1st March 1963.

Steam's heyday

Faster trains

Railway development was not standing still while BR faced up to the modernisation plan and the Beeching era. The regions were able to benefit from the civil engineering work that had brought the condition of main line tracks up to a standard capable of sustaining much faster running speeds than had obtained during the war. A succession of new or speeded-up express passenger trains was introduced on each region during this period, using steam locomotives. In the absence of the pre-war streamlined trains, the LMR and ScR nevertheless were able to launch the Caledonian, the fastest steam train to run post-war between London and Glasgow using Stanier Pacific power. On the east coast route, the challenge was met by the Elizabethan, non-stop between London and Edinburgh, taking advantage of the corridor tenders on selected A4 class locomotives to effect a crew change in motion. The WR introduced a new train, the Golden Hind, that ran faster to Plymouth behind 'King' class 4-6-0s than did the Cornish Riviera Express. On the SR the bi-hourly fast trains between Waterloo, Southampton, Bournemouth and Weymouth were speeded up despite their heavy loads of thirteen coaches, so that

Right: BR made simple improvements to many classes of steam locomotive during the late 1950s and early 1960s. The A3 Pacifics and some of the V2s of the east coast route received double Kylchap exhausts and new cylinders with improved steam flow. Modified A3 No. 60047 *Donovan* restarts an up express from Grantham station on 17th October 1960 as A4 No. 60022 *Mallard* hurries through with the down Flying Scotsman.

Above: As the result of experimental work done on the Swindon roller test plant and on controlled road tests, the WR was able to enhance the performance of its 'King' class 4-6-0s. Double-chimney 'King' No. 6002 *King William IV* arrives at Westbury on 10th October 1959 with the 9.30am from Paddington to Plymouth.

Below: A major rebuilding was scheduled for the Bulleid Pacifics of the Southern Region in view of a number of perceived design deficiencies. The first rebuilt 'Merchant Navy' class 4-6-2 No. 35018 *British India Line* had economically brought the down Bournemouth Belle Pullman train from Waterloo and was approaching Boscombe station near its journey's end on 21st May 1956.

the timing from Waterloo to Bournemouth was two hours dead, thu improving on the best pre-war timings all except one lighter weight business train. The SR's acquisition from 1941 onwards of a fleet of 140 Bulleid Pacific had made this possible.

The LMR speeded up Sheffield and Nottingham to St. Pancras services to nev levels, pushing the somewhat limited 'Jubilee' class locomotives to their limit, a indeed often using aged 2P 4-4-0s as pilot I should also mention the work done by the 'Britannia' 4-6-2s on the Liverpool Street-Norwich run on which a two-hou timing became possible when they were delivered, and by A4 Pacifics displaced l diesels to Scotland that did wonders wit the Glasgow-Aberdeen three-hour train

Improved locomotives

Neither did steam locomotive technical development stand still during this time In addition to the work done at the new Rugby steam locomotive testing plant that used rotating rollers driving dynamometers to measure locomotive performances, the older test plant at Swindon was put to good use by the enthusiastic team there led by S. O. Ell. Swindon's market niche was in maximising the steaming potential and output efficiency of existing locomotive designs. Arising from their work on tra forming the performance of the BR standard class 2 2-6-0s by adjustments t the blast pipe and chimney dimensions they also tested, among others, a ER V2 the BR 8P 4-6-2 *Duke of Gloucester*, a BR class 4 4-6-0 and a 9F 2-10-0 in the inter ests of performance improvement. It wa the splendid performance results they obtained with the former GWR 'Kings' and 'Castles' by upping their superheat and adding double chimneys that really drew public attention to their work. On the ER, even though it was relatively late in their lives, work proceeded on fitting the A3s and some of the V2s with new cylinders with outside steam pipes and better steam passages and double Kylchap exhausts. This gave these loco-

tives such a new lease of life that the
d A3s, newly adorned with German-
le half-depth smoke deflectors, gave
eral years of really sparkling perfor-
nces on the east coast main line.
e SR succeeded in obtaining funds for
uilding 90 of their Bulleid Pacifics on
re conventional lines. The result was in
s author's opinion a fleet of the finest
ific steam locomotives ever to run in
s country. If you doubt this, take a look
he internal layout of the sectioned loco-
tive No. 35029 next time you visit the
tional Railway Museum at York.

eyday

at this period was a heyday of steam is
hout doubt. Many locomotives were
e to show a clean pair of heels to the new
sel electrics introduced under the
dernisation plan. A 'Duchess', an A4 or a
uilt A3 had no problem in keeping the
ne timings that an English Electric Type 4
ot. A 'King' could equal a diesel hydraulic
arship' B-B. Neither did the five older
sels (10000, 10201 and their sisters) have
ything to spare on the 'Merchant Navy'
nedules on the SR. **END**

Above: The new exhaust arrangements on the Gresley A3s required smoke deflection to lift the exhaust clear of the driving cab windows, so new German-style smoke deflectors were fitted, as displayed on No. 60067 *Ladas* on 5th August 1961 as it passed Finsbury Park with the down Yorkshire Pullman.

Below: The 251 examples of the BR class 9F formed the largest standard class numerically and were probably the most successful of the BR standard types. No. 92009 has steam to spare as it climbs to the Trent Junction flyover with an iron ore train from Northamptonshire to Scunthorpe on 19th April 1963.

Corporate identity

New colours

To establish a new identity for British Railways, there had to be a complete break with the traditional railway image. The chosen medium was a set of colours and a lettering design that broke away from all previous styles used on the railways in the U.K.

In 1965 the BR Design Panel, supported by external consultants, proposed a base colour to be known as 'rail blue', a new mid-blue shade with a hint of green, that was not one of the colours listed in the British Standard. Two other colours were chosen, 'rail grey' which was a plain light grey, and 'flame red'.

Train liveries were to be based on rail blue. Passenger corridor coaches were to be painted overall rail blue with rail grey upper panels. All locomotives and non-corridor coaching stock vehicles were to be plain rail blue. Locomotive roofs would also be rail blue, but carriage roofs were to be painted a dark shade of grey. Underframes and bogies were at first painted an attractive shade of brown; a

Right: The BR corporate identity programme of 1965 made a complete break with all previous train liveries and lettering styles. The new identity was so successful that it was retained with little change for around 25 years. In 1974, rail blue class 40 diesel electric No. 40 051 leaves Lincoln St. Marks with a King's Cross to Grimsby and Cleethorpes train of blue-and-grey mark 2 stock.

Above: Apart from the Isle of Wight electrification which used second hand London Underground units painted rail blue, the SR's first major route scheme to employ the new BR corporate colours was that to Bournemouth and Weymouth. The plain blue of the REP+TC formations gave way to blue-and-grey on these units when they received their first repaints from 1968 onwards. In August 1968, 4-REP unit 3002 leads an up Bournemouth-Waterloo semi-fast into Eastleigh as a diesel electric multiple unit leaves the down platform for Southampton.

year later, workshop practice reverted to the inevitable daubed black.

Modern Pullman trains had the blue-and-grey applied in reverse, that is with the carriage in overall rail grey with a rail blue band across the window area. Most looked good in this style.

The paint used for rolling stock for the first few years had a semi-matt surface. The decision had been made to move away from multiple coats of paint and varnish, and to institute spray painting in those workshops where this could be practicably installed. The semi-matt surface made the all-blue carriages in particular look most dull.

Locomotives and multiple units already carried small yellow warning panels on their cab fronts. The new livery style extended the warning yellow area to cover the complete unglazed surface of each cab front.

Freight stock continued much as before, using grey for wagons without continuous brakes and bauxite brown for fitted wagons, except for the addition of a neat grouping of the principal numbers and lettering in white on a small, black-backed panel on the wagon side.

The railway road fleet of delivery vehicles and internal vans was to be painted bright yellow, with the lettering in black.

Lettering

BR commissioned a design for a standard typeface that met the modern vision for a clear, readable style using initial upper case and normal lower case letters. 'Rail alphabet' was close to Helvetica bold type as used by printers.

Symbol

Under the Railway Executive, BR had had two quite different badges, the lozenge-shaped plaque used in station platform nameplates, on the road cartage fleet and on letterheads; and the lion-over-wheel totem that handsomely graced locomotive tender and tank sides, and the sides of multiple unit power cars. The importance of badges had also not been lost on the BTC who, on the dissolution of the Railway Executive, had replaced the lion over-wheel with a less aesthetically satisfying lion-holding-wheel totem that had been taken from the top of the BTC's own heraldic device.

Above: Rail blue was used for all standard gauge locomotives other than steam, the final version including a complete all-over yellow cab front to enhance visibility from the trackside of approaching trains. Even Mr. Bulleid's first Co-Co d.c. electric locomotive No. 20001 received this livery for its final spell of life before withdrawal. It was seen at Eastleigh works after its last overhaul undergoing high voltage testing in February 1967.

Right: Each region in turn broke ranks and began to repaint formerly plain blue multiple units in blue-and-grey, the Scottish doing so from 1978 starting with the Inter-City class 126 units. Three such sets were photographed on 10th April 1982 near Barrhill on the 08.35 from Stranraer to Glasgow Central.

heraldry was not the image to be presented to the public to support the modern railway of the future, and the design for the double-arrow was a major move forward in this respect. The layout portrayed to some a double track passing through a junction. Some cynics said that it indicated that BR did not know which way it was going. The reality was that the double-arrow became widely recognised as the symbol for railways in this country. The double arrow was usually placed carefully in the livery design for each locomotive and multiple unit type. In railway applications it was arranged so that the upper arrow pointed right (i.e. viewed as a track plan, it represented left-hand running). The symbol formed the header

of all official letters, it was used in station exterior signs, and in all promotional material and advertising. The double arrow also appeared on the sides of railway-owned ferry funnels on a flame red background; in this application only was the "left-hand running" rule broken: the upper arrow always pointed to the bows of the ship.

Few changes

Through the years from 1965 surprisingly few changes were made officially to the new corporate train liveries. In the following decades all plain blue passenger-carrying coaches were progressively repainted in the two-tone style, a much more pleasing result. By the 1970s the paint type had been developed to a full gloss finish, and the appearance of trains was generally excellent.

The corporate identity liveries lasted for twenty five years. This period represented the quarter century of BR development under the structure of a central headquarters controlling the six or so regions through strong functional departments. This was a period when much progress was made in improving train services but when freight volumes tumbled, when management learned how to match long term changes in traffic volume with changes in capacity, when new stations began to be opened, and track, depot and facility rationalisation was carried out with energy. Twenty five years is probably too long for a corporate identity to remain. When the diesel high speed trains (HSTs or InterCity 125s) came on the scene in 1976 they looked distinctly odd in the "old clothes" colours borne more happily by older trains. More fundamental changes were soon to happen, which were to bring the idea of a corporate style to an end. 🔁

Above: The only BR steam locomotives expected to have a life beyond 1968 were the three 2ft gauge 2-6-2Ts on the Vale of Rheidol line in west Wales. These were the only steam locomotives to be painted BR rail blue. In this style, No. 9 was photographed on 28th January 1978 at Aberffrwd. *Colour-Rail*

Top Right: By reversing the corporate colours to grey-and-blue, a sleek style was adapted for the modern Pullman cars used on the east coast route, and on the diesel electric Pullman trains which by 1970 had gravitated on to the Western Region. The 09.00 Pullman service from Paddington to Cardiff and Swansea was photographed that year passing St. Fagans in South Wales.

Right: The grey-and-blue style did not suit older Pullman cars, for which BR's design panel insisted on a more *ersatz* adaptation of the standard blue-and-grey. The first to be so painted was Brighton Belle electric unit No. 3053 at Eastleigh in 1969.

The end of steam

The last new build orders

I have never satisfactorily understood why, three years after the introduction in 1957 of the first of the modernisation plan diesels, BR was still building steam loco-motives. Right until 1960, Swindon works continued to turn out class 9F 2-10-0s, admittedly the finest steam freight engines ever to run in this country. Indeed, Swindon was well into building the 'Warship' B-B diesel hydraulics which were being outshopped in parallel with new 9F 2-10-0s from the same works! Other batches of 9Fs came from Crewe works. It was probably only an accident of workshop production history that Swindon finished its final batch of 2-10-0s later than Crewe did theirs. With an eye to the historical nature of the event, the last steam locomotive built for British Railways, 9F 2-10-0 No. 92220, was given a GWR-style copper cap to its chimney, lined green livery, and the entirely appro-priate name *Evening Star*.

Southern reluctance

I remember reading somewhere that the SR did not plan to eliminate steam traction

Right: Two weeks before this photograph was taken, the SR had run two "last steam" specials for enthusiasts from London to Bournemouth and back. The planned last day of all SR steam was 9th July 1967. 'Merchant Navy' class 4-6-2 No. 35023, formerly named *Holland-Afrika Line*, was seen arriving at Bournemouth on 8th July 1967 with what railway management intended to be the final steam-worked Bournemouth to Waterloo train, hence the chalked inscription on the smoke box front. The next day a diesel loco-motive failure was the excuse needed for 35030 to work the final final steam train to Waterloo! *Alan Thorpe*

Steam's last fling

without compensating electrification of its main routes. While the electrification to Bournemouth together with diesel push-pull working of the Weymouth portions was planned for 1967, it was in some ways less clear how steam was to be eliminated from the Waterloo-Exeter main line. The SR appeared to want to go on running steam on that route until electrification could be accomplished. That would almost certainly have been a long and protracted case to make, taking BR into the early 1970s before there would be any hope of closing down the last steam depot. Faced with this seemingly resolute impasse on the part of the SR, the BRB in a decisive move effected its decision to transfer all SR routes west of Salisbury to the WR. The suddenness with which this was done surprised everybody. The announcement was made on the day of the transfer, and not even the SR general manager, we were told, knew in advance that it was going to happen.

The practical effect of this was that the WR was able to draft 'Warship' B-B diesel hydraulics to the Waterloo-Exeter service. This enabled steam traction to be cleared

from that line many years earlier than would otherwise have happened. The SR was able to use Hampshire diesel electric multiple units and Type 3 Bo-Bos on those trains from Reading and London that terminated at Salisbury.

Steam's last fling

On many routes, the knowledge that steam was to give way to other forms of traction prompted drivers to have one last fling before steam disappeared. I remember talk on the SR, for example, of drivers vying with each other to join the "ton club" as they pushed their powerful rebuilt 'Merchant Navy' class Pacifics up to and over 100mph on Bournemouth and Exeter expresses. 104mph in the down direction at Axminster seems to have been the best published top speed, equalling the record published for the unrebuilt version of the class.

Similar feats were happening on main lines all over the country. The ER and NER Pacifics produced some splendid runs as they used their high temperature super-

Above: The first BR standard locomotiv[e] to be withdrawn, after a life of less than eight years, was class 4 2-6-4T No. 80103 On 6[th] October 1962 it had already joine[d] a line of former Great Eastern 0-6-0s at Stratford for scrapping.

Right: With the withdrawal of steam loc[o]motives came the potential to demolish a[nd] sell off some of the depots and their sites. Structures such as heavy concrete coaling plants were not easy to clear. This one at Cricklewood in north London is providing coal for 9F 2-10-0 No. 92086.

heat and double chimney exhaust layou[t] to the full. A4s had a second last fling in Scotland as they ran a speedy and reliabl[e] service of trains between Glasgow and Aberdeen on a tight, three-hour timing. On the LMR the Stanier Pacifics had a les[s] sparkling end as they became demoted t[o] lower classified trains when English Electric Type 4 diesels took over the top expresses, but the 'Britannias', 'Royal Scots' and 'Jubilees' on the Midland mai[n] line put in some sparkling performances

Right: In the mid-1960s there was a spate of special trains for railway enthusiasts who wanted to experience steam locomotives working in unusual areas before the opportunity was lost for ever. 'Merchant Navy' class 4-6-2 No. 35003 *Royal Mail* reached Derby in 1963 with a Home Counties Railway Society excursion.

Below Right: On the North Eastern Region, pre-1923 Q6 0-8-0s, and J27 0-6-0s such as No. 65833 seen here at Sunderland depot, competently worked coal, steel and minerals trains around the north east industrial area until finally displaced by diesel traction.

before the BR/Sulzer Type 4 1Co-Co1s took over. Not to be outdone, ER and WR 9Fs were recorded on occasions on passenger trains at 90mph!

Fleet reductions

In retrospect we can see that events on the early BR occurred in the wrong order. I have already commented earlier in this book on the enthusiasm of the Railway Executive for building new steam locomotives instead of adopting a policy of going for new diesel and electric traction. Then to have built so many diesels of relatively untried types was an action that was compounded by the subsequent effects of Dr. Beeching's reshaping programme. BR ended up with far too many locomotives towards the end of the reduction in the BR network size and many steam and diesel locomotives had short lives.

In an ideal world, the Railway Executive would first have been charged with the task of deciding on the future size of the railway network, and of establishing a system to enable the network size to be adjusted in the face of subsequent changes in the transport market. Thereafter would have been the right time to replace steam traction without building any standard steam designs other than the 9Fs,

providing just enough electrics and diesels to serve a rationalised network, over a sufficient timescale to enable development of the right designs and sufficient training to ensure competence in the handling and maintenance of the new traction types. However, in the late 1940s and early 1950s, there was no clear vision that the whole transport scene was about to be thrown into change by the huge upsurge in road transport, and the railway chiefs of

the day can be forgiven for being optimistic about continuity of the *status quo.*

Diesel fleet changes

The one great advantage of the way things were actually done was that the surplus of diesel locomotives at the end of the Beeching era enabled BR to rid itself of the most unsuitable locomotives from the pil

Left: After steam had finished in 1968 scrap yards all over the country obtained them and began to cut them up. By far the biggest group was the two hundred or so that ended up at Barry Island in Woodham's yard, photographed in 1970.

Below Left: By not breaking up the majority of the condemned steam locomotives in his scrap yard at Barry, Dai Woodham managed to extend their existence into the period when private money began to become available for their purchase for .preservation. Both rebuilt 'West Country' 4-6-2 No. 34028 *Eddystone* and 'King' 4-6-0 No. 6024 *King Edward I* were to face a future in preservation, though not yet realised when seen at Barry in January 1972.

350hp 0-6-0 diesel electric type supplemented by the Drewry and BR/Gardner diesel mechanical 204hp 0-6-0s.

The end

Steam was first eliminated in the Great Eastern division of the ER, then in the WR as a whole and then in Scotland. The SR ran its last steam trains on 9th July 1967, running Pacific-hauled express trains on the Waterloo-Bournemouth-Weymouth line to the end. The northern part of the ER (the new, enlarged ER had been created by combining the former Eastern and North Eastern Regions a year or two earlier) had the privilege of keeping pre-grouping steam traction operating to its last day in the form of former North Eastern Railway 0-8-0s and 0-6-0s in the coal, steel and chemical producing Tyne and Tees areas. To the largest region, the (often explicitly stated) difficult-to-manage London Midland Region, fell the honour of running BR's last steam trains, in the Lancashire, Derbyshire and Cumbria areas. Some expensive-to-join special trains were run to commemorate the end of BR steam using the last operational BR class 7 4-6-2 *Oliver Cromwell* and a group of the erstwhile and popular Stanier class 5 4-6-0s. And that was that - or so we thought.

tches. Thus the Metro-Vick/Crossley o-Bo diesel electrics quickly disappeared, did the five A1A-A1A Type 4 diesel draulics that the WR had received from orth British. The NBL and AEI Type 1s d not last long either. There was some ubt about the performance of the Type 2 aby Deltics", but the robustness of their glish Electric pedigree suggested that ey had a future with some technical odifications. The class of ten was there-

fore refurbished and re-entered service for a relatively short time, only to be withdrawn following further traffic losses.
BR had purchased a similarly long list of types of diesel shunting locomotive. These also found less use as a result of the fall-off of freight traffic. Weeding out the non-standard types soon eliminated the less common classes. Thus, after all the blood-letting, shunting locomotive survivors were mainly of the BR standard

Centralising train design

At the time that the BR Workshops Plan came into effect in 1962, the railway workshops were removed from the jurisdiction of the regional chief mechanical and electrical engineers (CM&EEs) and placed under the Workshops Division, later to become BREL.

Soon afterwards, it became clear to the BRB's director of M&E engineering that traction and rolling stock design would be better focused if it was not left scattered around the regions in offices such as those at Brighton, London Bridge, Swindon, Doncaster, Crewe and Glasgow. Initiation of new train designs was already a central BRB function, and it was not sensible to have to farm out detail requirements to different offices around the country, whereas a central design centre would be able to deal with projects more effectively.

Thus was born the Railway Technical Centre (RTC) in Derby. Purpose-built on a "brown field" site, the modern office block complex was opened in 1967. It attracted not only the centralised M&EE function including the train design offices, but also became home for BR Research which was set up for fundamental research into all aspects of railway engi-

Left: During the late 1960s BR took steps to close down the regional train design offices and concentrate the work at the Railway Technical Centre in Derby. One of the last new locomotive types to be designed with strong regional characteristics was the Southern Region 1,600/600hp electro-diesel type that became class 73. In August 1979 one of these most reliable of locomotives approaches Bromley South with the overnight Night Ferry train from Paris and Brussels to London Victoria.

Left: Centralised research and design enabled progress to be made on developing high speed suspensions. The prototype high speed diesel train (HST) was one result from this. The train is seen passing through Doncaster station during trials in 1973.

Below: The BR Research team were given their head to design a 250km/h tilting train that would embrace many concepts new to railways. After successful running of the gas turbine-powered experimental advanced passenger train (APT), three prototype long 25kV electric trains were built at Derby, and allocated to the Scottish Region for service between Glasgow and London Euston. On 19th November 198? units 373 001 and 373 006 arrived at Carlisle on a trial working from Glasgow. Bo-Bo electric No. 87 006 *City of Glasgow* called with a more conventional Glasgow-Euston service (right).

...ering. In time, the Railway Technical ...ntre attracted many associated M&E ...gineering support groups including ...entific services, a central purchasing ...m, a group library, rail vehicle testing, a ...hicle development workshop, and ...otographic and documentation ...vices. At its most heavily populated ...riod the RTC complex housed over ...00 people.

...an adjunct to the research and vehicle ...ting work carried out at the RTC, the ...B set up a test track at Old Dalby on the ...osed main line that used to link ...ottingham with Kettering via Melton ...owbray. BR Research and other groups ...veloped a collection of laboratory ...aches and test vehicles, in some cases ...wered by dedicated locomotives or ...esel railcars.

...uch good work originated in the RTC. ...R Research in particular generated funda- ...ental understanding into the behaviour ...rail vehicle suspensions, based on ...search into the rail/wheel interface. ...veral successful products arose from ...s work. The excellent riding bogies of ...odern BR multiple unit stock owe their ...nesis to the BR Research work. The idea ...at evolved into the two-axle 'Pacer' ...oup of low cost railbuses came from ...search into freight vehicle suspensions. ...d a series of innovative design features ...veloped by BR Research came together ...the advanced passenger train (APT), ...table as the world's most advanced ...say into the possibility of using tilting ...ins to shorten journey times on existing ...lway tracks.

...parallel with all this work, the M&EE ...sign team, using an up-to-date amalgam ...more conventional design wisdom, ...oduced the prototype diesel electric ...gh speed train (HST). This incorporated ...sign of a lightweight power car using the ...tent Paxman Valenta diesel engine and ...aking the first use on BR of rotating ...odes to avoid the need for alternator ...mmutation; and the new BR mark 3 ...ach with surely the best and most ...onomical steel carriage body design ...er. The HST fleet remains the world's ...stest diesel fleet at 125mph maximum ...erating speed. **END**

Top: Research to develop a higher speed freight wagon suspension produced additional fruit in the form of a two-axle railbus prototype. This was foreseen as a potential low-cost replacement for ageing diesel multiple units. The first Leyland experimental vehicle, LEV1, was photographed at the premises of the Railway Technical Centre in Derby in 1982.

Above: Opened in 1967, the Railway Technical Centre enabled concentration of most BR HQ mechanical and electrical engineering activities in one location. At its peak there were over 2,000 people employed on the site.

Down with divisions

Life in a division

In order to manage its large and complex self, BR had developed a pyramid organisation pattern. A central BR headquarters, mostly located in London at 222 Marylebone Road, headed up six (later five) regions, each of which managed their areas through a group of divisional organisations. To illustrate the role of a division more clearly I can describe how it appeared to me in the early 1970s when I occupied the post of traction maintenance engineer in the Doncaster division of the ER. The Doncaster division covered the combined area of the former Doncaster and Hull divisions of the old ER and NER. The day-to-day performance of the railway was monitored from the divisional headquarters building at Gresley House. The divisional manager was responsible for appointing and managing the area managers and, in conjunction with the appropriate regional headquarters engineers, the divisional engineers. The divisional management team was set performance targets to meet for improved performance in each manager's field of influence. In my case that meant attempting to balance traction reliability and daily availability with the costs of maintenance at the depots, and to obtain annual improvements in each of these. During my time at Doncaster division we made important economies in staff numbers at Hull Botanic Gardens d.m.u. depot (with the

Right: There was a lot of input from the management of the ER's Doncaster Division to the successful implementation in 1974 of the iron ore tippler trains for the British Steel Corporation's new flow of imported iron ore from Immingham docks to the steelworks at Scunthorpe. In this view at the Immingham loading point, two class 37 Co-Cos head a 2,100 ton train of 100 ton BSC bogie tipplers.

Above: This scene at Market Rasen in the Doncaster Division shows what can happen when a wagon axlebox runs hot, sufficiently hot to melt the axle journal. The divisional engineer's task was two-fold: to ensure proper and safe arrangements were put in hand to clear the line and restore it to traffic; and to assist the operator to determine the full cause of the derailment.

M&EE work study team at ER HQ in York providing the expert calculations) in parallel with improvements to train reliability. We introduced lubricating oil centrifuging to clean and recycle dirty locomotive sump oil at Immingham (a depot initiative), and made the best use of the pitted facility at Doncaster depot for fleet modification work. Lincoln d.m.u. depot was always regarded highly by the Doncaster divisional engineers, having the task of maintaining what were then BR's oldest surviving diesel railcars in the form of the class 114 Derby heavyweight two-car sets.

The ER, in common with other regions, had adopted a form of cost accounting that enabled us to know the cost of maintaining each class of traction and rolling stock type of vehicle, month by month, at each depot. We could see which depots cost more than others, which were the more expensive traction types (did you know that the depot costs of a three-car d.m.u. were as high as those of a class 47?) and how well labour was utilised. It was by using cost data from this system that the BRB's CM&EE decided against diesel hydraulic locomotives in favour of diesel electrics. Senior divisional operators and engineers (such as myself) had to share an on-call roster to advise or attend derailments and serious incidents on the railway. This was where I learned the fascinating task of determining the causes of derailments, of seeking out the small marks on the rail head of wheel treads or flanges that told their story of what had actually happened an hour or two earlier. The responsibility for agreeing the cause of a serious derailment on the main line rested with the divisional people. When we were baffled we could call on the specialists from BR Research to unravel scientifically the mysteries of vehicle dynamics. We also had to plan the attendance of the appropriate breakdown train, crane or cranes and ensure safe working on the site. During my time I was impressed by the professionalism of the breakdown train teams that came from the depots. I would commend the Doncaster depot team of that period particularly highly.

The more difficult derailments, or those incidents which led to loss of life or limb, required an internal inquiry to be set up, usually chaired by the divisional operating manager with other managers and engineers on the panel. We had to be something of a mixture of railway experts personnel counsellors and detectives to get

ove: When the class 47-propelled mark 3 push-pull trains were placed in service, Scottish Regional management made special efforts to ef staff to encourage a successful service launch. On 12th June 1981, Co-Co No. 47 712 *Lady Diana Spencer* stands at Glasgow Queen eet with the 07.30 to Edinburgh Waverley.

he bottom of some of the root causes of idents and incidents on our patch of way. So, by the time I was asked if I uld consider applying for a job in otland, I had amassed some valuable nds-on railway management experience.

cotland first

he mid 1970s, the BRB was moving vards the idea that the divisional layer management represented an on-cost t could be eliminated. The proposal s that the regional general managers d their headquarters people could nage strategy, monitoring of the areas d "control" of train services. More ponsibility for day-to-day workings uld be taken on by the area managers

and area engineers. The regional engineering functions would take on the role of the divisional engineers. Areas would be made larger by combining adjacent areas together.

The guinea pig for all this was the smallest region on BR, the Scottish Region. By the time I worked there from 1976 its divisions had all gone, and the ScR HQ managers and engineers managed the railway and its stations and depots through the area managers and engineers directly.

Major changes

The late 1970s and early 1980s was a period of great change for the railways in Scotland and elsewhere. We were preparing for the allocation to

Craigentinny depot of HSTs for the east coast main line, and to Shields and Polmadie depots in Glasgow of the three APT production trains for the west coast route. Other new or improved depot facilities were in hand at Ayr, Motherwell, Aberdeen Clayhills, Corkerhill and Inverness.

The scheme to replace the mark 2 double-locomotive push-pull trains on the Edinburgh-Falkirk-Glasgow run was ScR inspired, but fully supported by BR HQ. The mark 3 trains with class 47/7 locomotives enabled the Region to promise a step change in quality of service. The general manager insisted that all staff taking part in the operation of the revised service must be briefed personally by their supervisors as each stage of preparation for the new service was reached, so that by the day of

launch everyone was keyed up to
ke a success of it. In that first day, time-
eping, which had been below 40% right
ne in the weeks before, rocketed to well
er 90%, and on some days in the next
onths it reached 100% right time!
ot everything was positive. At the
eneral manager's meetings, particularly
hen budgets were under discussion,
ere was considerable pressure on all of
to go on reducing costs. I had to lead a
mber of area maintenance engineers
ough the difficult, and sometimes
inful, process of closing depots, a move
ancially preferable to reducing staffing
several depots. We closed depots at
indee and Hamilton (d.m.u.s) and
wnhill (wagons).

arket led

ntrary to many people's perceptions,
e railway was very much market led,
her than engineer led. When Chris
een was in Scotland as regional general
inager there were many market-led
tiatives. A concerted effort to publicise
e railway led to the name "Scotrail" being
nceived, later rewritten as "ScotRail".
e advent of bus deregulation in the
K., and the presence of many new bus
erators in Scotland with routes between
jor cities, required a railway response.
otRail (as the region had become known
ne name has since stuck!) confronted
s competition innovatively with a series
fare offers. The region launched a new
sh-pull, low-fare Inter-City service
tween Edinburgh and Inverness using
e maintenance spare train set, and a
imber of the bus routes disappeared.
otRail later extended push-pull opera-
n to the Glasgow and Edinburgh to
erdeen and Inverness trains under the
nner 'ScotRail Express'.
ring the five years from 1980 to 1984,
ssenger receipts in Scotland rose by
%, not quite enough to beat inflation
t disguising a sharp dip in 1982 that was
lowed by a strong recovery.
nctuality improved right across the
iod. Freight volume collapsed in
rallel with all BR, as coal burning in

Scottish power stations gave way to
nuclear energy and oil, and as general
freight declined. To counter the effects of
the traffic volume changes, the region
made major reductions in staff (15%) and
route miles (5%) of railway. The advent of
four new power signalling centres enabled
mechanical signalboxes across the region
to be reduced by 55 (24%)[9].
In these ways ScotRail tried to keep abreast
of the rate of change of traffic volume.
I believe we were not "deeply inefficient" at
this time, though it was often a struggle to
keep up with changes in national traffic
trends which equally affected cross-border
traffic to and from England.

Above: Scottish Region opened a number
of new depots during the late 1970s and
early 1980s. This one for diesel multiple
units inspections at Corkerhill in Glasgow
was funded by the local authority who
wanted the site of some badly-arranged
carriage sidings for a road scheme.

Left: A Scottish Region initiative
persuaded the BR mechanical and electric
engineering headquarters to provide electric train heat capability on class 37
locomotives, thus enabling the elimination
of steam heating on trains in the Highlands,
the last such outpost on BR. With the Isle of
Skye in the background, No. 37 416 stands
at Kyle of Lochalsh in 1985 with the afternoon train to Inverness.

Model for future

I believe the Scottish Region example showed clearly how much more respon sive the railway could be to market tren when general management was not sep rated from the running railway by the la of divisional management. This is not to say that the larger regions would find life as readily manageable as did ScotRail. E the BRB was clearly convinced, because divisions were closed down in the next year or two, even on large regions like th ER and LMR.

Above: The conversion of three surplus class 25 diesel locomotives into train supply generator vehicles was undertaken entirely by Scottish Region engineers and depot staff. Co-Co No. 37 085 leads 97 252 at Glasgow Queen Street after arrival with the Fort William to Euston sleeping car train on 20th October 1983.

Below: Close relationships between regional management and local authorities were essential to the success of the increasing number of railway developments funded by local authorities. On the London Midland Region, 'Pacer' unit No. 142 002 calls at Shaw on 5th October 1985 with the 14.25 from Manchester Victoria to Rochdale via Oldham. *Mrs. Mary Boocock.*

Left: As part of the ever-continuous drive to reduce costs, concentration of maintenance of diesel multiple units on fewer locations in Scotland enabled the depots at Dundee and Hamilton to be closed. The stark emptiness of Hamilton depot was photographed in October 1982, soon after its demise.

Below: Scottish Region initiatives included the adoption of the term ScotRail, and the introduction of the low-fare Jacobite train from Edinburgh to Inverness to counter road bus competition following bus deregulation. In summer 1984, the Jacobite, formed of the maintenance spare push-pull set propelled by a class 47/7, heads through the highlands towards Aviemore.

Down with costs

Work study

Building on Dr. Beeching's vision, BR had embraced the principles of work study with great enthusiasm. Managers, supervisors and practitioners were sent on intensive training courses, and quickly learned the two key "steps to efficiency": method study, wherein the way a job is done is studied and revised to reduce the time and effort required; and work measurement, wherein the resultant revised method, having been implemented, is timed in detail. Hand in hand with work study ran the possibility of using the timings to form a basis for bonus payments to the staff. All regions became involved with work study, under different management philosophies. Probably the most enthusiastic at the detail end of the spectrum was the LMR.

Rationalisation

The WR had a somewhat more objective approach. That region frequently took a top-down look at what was happening, and asked itself the question, "Need this be done at all?" Then, rather than cut into staff

Right: The need to adapt train lengths to the business available on the Hull-Liverpool Trans-Pennine diesel multiple unit service had led to the reduction in train lengths from six to five cars by the removal of one of the two centre trailer vehicles. A later, further economy of some significance was made by the Eastern Region when one of the four power cars in each set was converted to a trailer car without affecting the trains' ability to keep time. One of the five-car class 124 sets, still then operating with all eight engines, was photographed on a Liverpool to Hull working in 1975 approaching Broomfleet on BR's longest section of straight track.

Left: The Western Region pursued a relentless programme of track and siding rationalisation that left a legacy requiring timely train operation to avoid serious delays at some locations. One such route was the Salisbury to Exeter line which had been singled over long lengths in the late 1960s. The class 50 English Electric 2,700 Co-Cos proved to be a reliability challenge even when heavily refurbished. One of the modified locomotives, No. 50 027 *Lion*, is seen on the single line near Tisbury on 18 October 1986 with the 07.00 Waterloo-Exeter. *Brian Morrison*

numbers at all locations all round the region, it systematically closed down those parts of the network that could be dispensed with. The WR attitude was to cut and cut "until the pips squeaked". Thus many, many routes were singled, including long lengths of the Salisbury-Exeter line and the main line in Cornwall; lots of

branch lines, yards, sidings and passing loops were rationalised. South Wales railways were severely reduced during this period, the late 1960s and early 1970s. Crossovers were taken out if the basic service could be worked without them. At the end of all that, then the detailed work study work was done to bring the

staff levels to those needed to run the rationalised railway. This was certainly not a "deeply inefficient" way of managing. I remember, from my period working on the WR, that we found some diesel traction depots to be working at astonishingly low work performance levels. There were wide variations across the region. The WR did eventually catch up with other regions in depot productivity, but the cost of the previous lack of performance and over-manning had been to price the diesel hydraulics out of the market as far as the BRB's chief M&E engineer was concerned.

All other regions rationalised their railways, too, though sometimes not so severely as the WR. I remember, on my

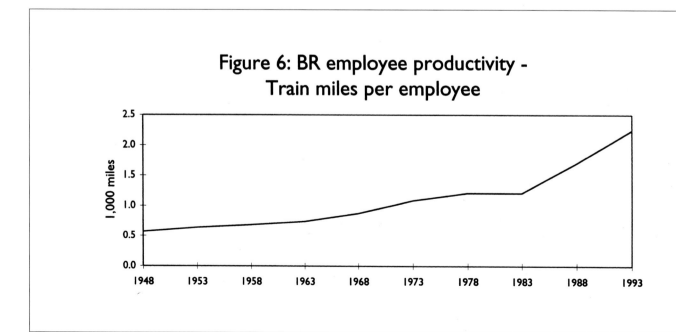

Figure 6: BR employee productivity - Train miles per employee

bove: This grand station is at Pontypridd in South Wales, once a busy centre providing steam locomotive-hauled connections for ssengers in several directions. The simpler train services that the WR provided with d.m.u.s in the Cardiff valleys needed much less track d station capacity. In September 1971 a train for Barry Island waits in the bay. The up platform track had long since been removed.

elow: The director M&EE used a nation-wide depot costing system to compare the overhaul and maintenance costs of similar diesel comotives. In this comparison the WR class 52 C-C diesel hydraulic locomotives came out badly in the light of lower national costs for ass 47 diesel electrics and so were listed for early withdrawal. One of the class 52s heads west away from Cardiff past St. Fagans in 1970 th a train of empty mark 1 passenger stock.

Above: As the rest of the south Manchester electric suburban services had been electrified at 25kV, the 1,500V d.c. Hadfield route was converted to 25kV a.c., the final work being done by closing the line for just one weekend. The erstwhile class 506 units, like the one illustrated leaving Ashburys on 7th June 1984, were replaced by class 303 units that had been displaced by rationalisation of train working in the Strathclyde area, thus avoiding the cost of new units.

Below: One feature of railway life that was perhaps a commentary on human nature was the way in which civil engineers' wagons were often perceived to fill up freight yards that had been released as not needed for commercial freight operations. On 28th April 1981, Scottish Region BRCW/Sulzer Bo-Bo No. 27 027 passed Greenhill Lower with a train of ballast wagons that it had probably collected from Larbert for a track maintenance job the coming weekend.

arrival in a senior post on the LMR in 198[being surprised at how much surplus tra[and overhead line metalwork was still in place in the former GCR yards around m[new work base at Manchester. The WR, ER and ScR, when I worked on them, ha[vigorously pursued the lifting for sale or re-use of all surplus track and ironmongery. This was just one element which supported some railway managers' view that the LMR was a little too large to manage successfully.

Reorganisations

In the 1980s there was in British management a strong view that many problems control could be resolved by reorganisin[the management structure. BR was not immune from that. Most reorganisation[up till then had been aimed at saving ove[head costs by removing a layer of management, such as the elimination of districts in the 1950s and the divisions in the early 1970s. Following chapters in th[book trawl over the effects of later BR red ganisations that built up the railway businesses and removed the regions. These changes had different objectives: they were not specifically for cost cutting they were for improving management focus and making the railway more customer-oriented.

Continuous pressure

All the time, the pressure for cost reduction was continuous. Traffic was still being lost to road and air transport, and railway capacity and management costs had to be cut ruthlessly even just to keep pace. It is very much more difficult to make sufficient cuts in a middle level of management when your outfit has to pay the costs of a large headquarters that is no[itself downsizing in accordance with the change in traffic income.

Seen from the outside, particularly from the point of view of politicians and the Treasury, the railways were still losing money, the losses did not reduce, and thu[BR was vulnerable to political interferenc[

Objectives

During Sir Richard Marsh's tenure as chairman of BRB, he made great play with his view that the government, represented by the Minister of Transport, should set clear objectives for BR. Was it to be a business and be slimmed so as to cost the taxpayer less? (Sir Richard actually believed that national railways could never be profitable.[10]) Or should the railways be considered as performing a social service, a role which did not preclude them being run on business lines, but one for which the country, that is the government, that is the taxpayer, would have to be prepared to pay? The 1968 Transport Act had partially addressed this issue by separating out those unprofitable passenger routes designated as socially necessary, and by allocating grants to them. This did not work for long in the face of the severe inflation of the Wilson Labour government period in which fares did not keep up with cost increases. BR, working without clear objectives, soon declined into severe loss.

The next chairman of BRB, that great motivator of people, Sir Peter Parker, decided that, in the absence of any clear government objectives for BR, the BRB would write its own objectives and submit them for approval by the government. He laid down some basic principles, that is the BRB would assume that the revenue subsidy for BR in each of the coming years would be at the same level as the current year, adjusted for inflation, and that investment cash would be available in much the same quantity as before. The BRB also assumed that the size of the railway would not change, that the country wanted the railway to be about the current size. BR would manage within these limits. The government went along with this approach to objective setting, and thus BR was for a time free to continue in the knowledge that no great changes were expected to the railway system.

However, when a body such as a railway is dependent on a government for cash year on year, there always comes a time, sooner or later, when the government wants to reduce the cash demand. Many more changes lay waiting for BR in the years ahead. ■

Above: As chairman of the British Railways Board, Sir Peter Parker will be remembered as a great motivator, popular with management and personnel generally. He was able to stem BR's decline into serious loss-making, and laid foundations for the railways' recovery over the next decade by setting demanding financial objectives and actively encouraging their achievement. *British Rail*

Ships and hotels: out

Overseas connections

All round the coasts of island Great Britain there were ferries to foreign and not so foreign parts. From the meagre Isle of Wight paddle steamers to the large overnight motor vessels on the Harwich to Hoek van Holland crossing, British Railways owned a sizeable majority of them. This network of ferries was part of a greater routeing strategy linking trains with ships, and using strategically placed, good hotels as staging points.

Travel changes

These railway ships and hotels survived nationalisation and became part of British Railways. As travel patterns changed in favour of air and road transport, the shipping lines and the hotels had to seek different or smaller markets. Railway management was already being hard pressed by the challenge of restructuring the railways themselves to counter the effects of vigorous competition from the other transport modes. The ships and hotels were, frankly, a diversion, and, though not loss-making, they were becoming a burden that was outside the experience of railway managers who could not respond adequately to their new market needs. The government view was that railwaymen should run railways, and that the ships and hotels should be sold to companies that were

Right: British Railways' portfolio of shipping routes included cross-Channel ferries as well as those to off-shore British islands and on cross-estuary routes. The BR motor vessel *Southsea* was one of three that provided a direct connection between the Isle of Wight railways at Ryde and the main line link from Portsmouth Harbour to London Waterloo.

Above: A penalty for maintaining rail and shipping links was the need for rail links to harbours in locations that were difficult of access. For example, badly parked cars often obstructed the Waterloo-Weymouth Quay boat train as is seen in this view of Sulzer Typ 3 Bo-Bo No. 33 119 on 26th July 1983. A policeman has to remove a Vauxhall Viva from t path of the train before passengers could reach the ferry.

Left: The North British Hotel broods over Edinburgh's main railway station amid the Waverley gardens in 1975 as a class 40 1 Co-Co1 passes through the cutting with a block freight train of Presflo cement wagons. BR had sold off most of the hotels to private owne by the early 1980s.

already in those particular disciplines and thus able to concentrate expert resources and cash on them.

By this time, BR had been successfully marketing the ferries under the 'Sealink' name, and had ventured also into the Isle of Wight and cross-Channel hovercraft business with its innovative Seaspeed subsidiary. Sealink was therefore sold, with the Scandinavian firm Stena taking the major portion. Buyers were also found for the hovercraft routes.

Some ferry companies were subsequently sold on to firms that could invest in replac ment vessels. Noteworthy was the Portsmouth-Ryde service that changed completely from large motor ships to the faster, more utilitarian catamarans that skim across to the Isle of Wight today und Wightlink ownership while still maintaining train connections at both ends.

Above: BR provided a faster alternative to ships for the crossings from the Isle of Wight to Southampton and to Southsea using SRN6 hovercraft. Its subsidiary Seaspeed also ran large SRN4 hovercraft across the English Channel. All were sold off, though the Southampton route proved short-lived. This view shows an SRN6 hovercraft coming ashore alongside the Woolston "floating bridge" at Southampton in 1967.

otels

contrast to the ships, BR sold most of
e hotels individually to many different
yers who, one by one, were able to put
w capital into them and to raise their
ndards. The links with the railways
re severed, each hotel generally being
veloped as a city centre hotel aimed at
e business and higher-spending
mmunities. Many former railway
tels lost their old names and changed
ntities completely. Some, like the fine
d Adelphi Hotel in Liverpool, did retain
t only their names but their style,
ilding on the grand traditions that
cades in railway ownership had given
em. Such hotels retain a grandeur and a
esence that is rare today.

vesting themselves of the ships and
tels started a series of changes on BR.
her specialist functions found them-

selves being separated and trimmed for
sale. Travellers Fare, at least that part
which ran the station buffets and kiosks,
went into the private sector, successfully
to become a higher quality retail food
outlet. But the many subsequent sales are
part of a much later story. 🔵

The business culture

M&EE first

When people say that a railway is "engineering led" they do not usually mean it as a complement. They imply that engineers are only interested in developing their hardware and pursuing their own interests, which leads to a railway that concentrates on running trains and which is not responsive to its customers' needs and wants. On the other hand, we are told, "market led" managers have the interests of the railway's customers at heart, and generally this is true. Yet one of the greatest revolutions in the organisation of railways in this country began as a result of action by its engineers.

The BRB's director of M&E engineering realised that the traction and rolling stock needs of the different railway train service groups were becoming polarised into generically exclusive types of train. Put simply, suburban and secondary passenger services were all heading towards using only multiple unit stock, the Inter-City trains were formed of air-conditioned carriages designed for 100mph running and upwards, and freight trains determined the tractive effort of diesel locomotives and were unique in using wagons. Thus the idea evolved to split up the traction and rolling stock personnel of the M&EE department of BR into three specialist groups: Inter-City, suburban, and freight, and to allocate responsibility for specific traction and rolling stock types to them. The three teams set up in 1979 were responsible for translating the BRB's passenger marketing plans into rolling stock designs and modifications. This time the modifications were as much for marketing reasons as for engineering reliability.

Over the years that followed, traction and rolling stock reliability improved. Nowadays delays to railway traffic come more from infrastructure-related problems than from the trains. I am convinced that the business structure of the M&EE traction and rolling stock activity was the inspiration that enabled this major and most positive change.

New business sectors

The business philosophy quickly caught on in BR. Five business sectors were set at BRB headquarters, specifically to focu on the markets for each sector, to promo

les, to identify revenues and costs, and plan strategically for the future of their ctor of railway development. The ctors were: InterCity; London & South st (L&SE); Other Provincial Services; ilfreight; and Parcels.

The business sectors gained strength in charting the direction that the railways were to take in the future. Yet working in management during this period of the early 1980s was not easy. Organisationally BR was divided into six

Above: By branding the HSTs 'Inter-City 125' BR put an extra level of prestige on an already popular product. An HST set accelerates along the cliff tops at Burnmouth on 23rd April 1984 working the 11.00 Inter-City service from London King's Cross to Edinburgh. *Mrs. Mary Boocock*

regions (the ER had lately given birth to Anglia Region); a number of strong functional departments, especially the engineering and operating functions and the major projects division; and the five business sectors. Almost all of these interfaced with each other.

The BRB chairman at this time, the first Sir Robert Reid, delighted to call the effects of all these interfaces a form of "constructive tension". Some of us read management textbooks to learn more about how to make things happen in a matrix organisation. It was a positive period in which the strong survived.

In the end, though, something had to give. Was it to be the regions, or the functions? We did not have to wait long to find out.

Expensive train maintenance

While all this fundamental change was developing, the BRB expressed great concern at the perceived high cost of maintaining trains. Traditionally, locomotives carriages and wagons had been overhauled in main works at intervals of a few years, and then maintained and serviced at depots on the regions. Diesel and electric

Above: The London & South East (L&SE) sector received deliveries of new class 455 electric multiple units for suburban services out of Waterloo and Victoria. Some of these replaced class 508 sets that were being transferred to Liverpool area services. One batch of 455s took over one trailer car from each displaced class 508 unit, as seen by the different profile of the second vehicle in unit 5719, photographed at Waterloo on 26th June 1985.

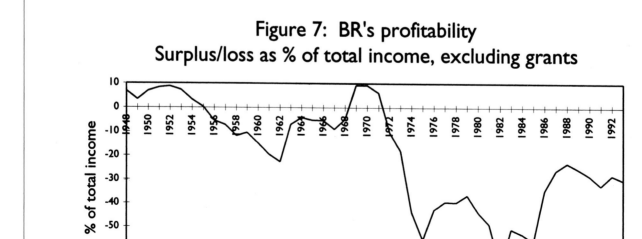

Figure 7: BR's profitability
Surplus/loss as % of total income, excluding grants

omotives received effectively the same
ic treatment at main works as had
am traction before them. The depots
d to have spare vehicles to put into
vice when others were under mainte-
ice or away at works.

ese arrangements kept the railway
ning, but only if availability could be
d at between 65-80% according to the
e of vehicle, meaning that at any time
re was 20-35% of the fleet stopped for
jineering attention. The assets were not
ng used effectively, and train mainte-
ice accounted for up to a quarter of all
way costs.

roject to improve

e BRB charged David Blake, director
&E engineering in the mid-1980s, with
proving matters. His study team
luded a number of experienced railway
jineers supported by consultants. My
t in this project was to propose, jointly
h a competent engineering consultant,
inges in the way trains were overhauled
I maintained. Under the project name
st-effective maintenance' (CEM) we
pposed, among much else, that where
ssible the overhaul of significant
mponents should be "unhooked" from
interval at which the vehicle body was
erhauled, each worn component being
changed for an overhauled one at depot
intenance between operating diagrams
overnight. This would enable
iximum use to be obtained from each
mponent, and would minimise vehicle
ie out of service.

vehicle overhauls or bogie changes, we
I observed a practice at the SR depot of
art Leacon near Ashford that would set
future model for elsewhere. Four-car
ctric multiple units were received on
e track, disconnected from their eight
gies, lifted off them by overhead crane,
I swung over to be united with a set of
ht overhauled bogies on the adjacent
ck. That work took one shift of about
ht hours. Pre-testing and final testing
bled the train usually to return to traffic
hours after it had been taken out.
e Chart Leacon principle was tailored to

HST and locomotive-hauled InterCity
train set overhauls at works such as Derby
and Wolverton. HST power cars got the
component exchange treatment at Neville
Hill, Bristol Bath Road and Laira.
Doncaster came up subsequently with an
excellent scheme that turned a two-car
Sprinter d.m.u. round on newly overhauled bogies in a weekend, with no time
out of weekday revenue-earning traffic!
We also developed works and depot rationalisation proposals that led to the
splitting of British Rail Engineering
Limited (BREL) into two chunks, heavy
overhaul works, and CEM depots. The
latter embraced works such as Glasgow
(renamed Springburn), Wolverton,
Eastleigh and Doncaster in a new group
called British Rail Maintenance Ltd.
(BRML). Separate from BRML but compli-
mentary to it were the business-owned
Level 5 depots such as those at Chart
Leacon, Stratford and Ilford.
My consultant friend and I proposed
much leaner organisations for the BRML
works and headquarters than they enjoyed
under BREL direction. One BREL executive stated confidently that it was
absolutely reasonable for the company to

Above: The first electric trains on the Isle
of Wight were redundant London
Underground Piccadilly line trains that
dated from between 1922 and 1930.
Twenty years after electrification, and then
part of the London & South East sector, a
train from Shanklin is seen arriving at Ryde
Pier Head on 25th May 1987.

employ one man on non-production work
for every direct production worker. We
disagreed, and the slimmed organisations
proved the point when BRML was set up.

Savings

Our report suggested that real cash savings
of around £30 million per year would result
from whole-hearted implementation of
this scheme. David Blake drew me to one
side about three years later and told me that
BR had just about doubled that saving.
I include this episode to illustrate how BR
had set its face against inefficiency and was
making strenuous efforts to tackle each
area of perceived "fat", prioritising those
with the greatest apparent scope for
improvement. Other engineering func-

tions were tackling similar productivity schemes, and the regions were successfully achieving positive productivity improvements each year. The business sectors were going all out for increased revenue. Margaret Thatcher, as prime minister, had for some years been praising the first Sir Robert Reid as "BR's excellent chairman" (her words), and there was no talk of anything resembling a railway that was "deeply inefficient" (except, perhaps, among those charged with sorting out wagonload freight). Figure 7 shows that the decline in BR's financial fortunes was arrested at this time, and the stage was set for improvements in the late 1980s. (Figure 7 data have been normalised as far as is reasonably practicable, to take account of the different phases of financial accounting and railway organisation.) ▪

Top Left: The Parcels sector began to pull together a somewhat disparate business into one with clear objectives. 25kV a.c. Bo-Bo No. 85 009 approaches Carlisle with a parcels train from London to Stranraer on 20th November 1982.

Bottom left: Freight entered a positive period when sectorised. BRCW/Sulzer Type 2 No. 26 001 heads an Inverness-bound mixed freight on the Highland main line near Tomatin in October 1979.

Top Right: The unpopularity of the two-axle 'Pacer' diesel multiple units led to the development for the Provincial Services sector of the bogie 'Sprinter' sets, more conventional replacements for BR's ageing d.m.u.s. These used diesel engine/transmission combinations that had proved reliable in continental railway service. Sprinter No. 150 129, leaves Duffield on 26th August 1987 on a Matlock to Derby working.

Bottom Right: The Provincial Services sector upgraded its principal trans-Pennine services with refurbished mark 2 sets hauled by class 47 Co-Co diesel electrics. No. 47 477 approaches York on 4th July 1987 with the 13.50 from Liverpool Lime Street to Newcastle Central.

Freight: snakes and ladders

The decline

I doubt if many people play the board game 'snakes and ladders' nowadays. But snakes and ladders is a perfect illustration of the frustrations of trying to keep a railway freight business afloat in a situation where bulk traffic in train loads is promising good returns but where wagonload traffic is leaking away to other forms of transport.

Rationalisation

Faced with a sharp decline in coal carryings in the north of England as general prosperity led to the advance of natural gas heating in homes, BR sought to close one of the three routes that crossed the Pennines between Yorkshire and the Manchester area. Since most coal had been carried on the Woodhead route, a route that had very little local passenger traffic, and on which major cable renewals were needed, that route was selected for closure. Through passenger trains and what freight was left could be re-routed. Thus the Woodhead line closed in July 1981. Even actions as bold as that did little enough to stem the financial disaster that was threatening BR's freight operations.

Railfreight sector

It so happened, however, that the Railfreight sector was one of the more vigorous business units set up by the BR. Strong management at the top led to revised strategies and a sharper focus of the sales force into the key product groupings, particularly for traffic that was carried on bulk, single-product trains. Sub-sectors were set up for coal, aggregates, petroleum products, chemicals, steel and general freight. The latter posed the biggest problem. The option to follow Ireland's lead and put all less-than-train-load loads on to container trains was not available to BR because the carriage of containers was Freightliners' job and Freightliners Ltd. was now part of the National Freight Corporation. Almost in desperation, Speedlink was born.

Above: The down-side of freight at this time was the desperate need to reduce costs. An extreme measure was the closure of the electri- Woodhead route across the Pennines. In this view taken in 1975, 1,500V d.c. Bo+Bos Nos. 76 012 and 76 006 head a westbound ded MGR coal train for Fiddler's Ferry power station.

ft: The Scottish Region assisted the Railfreight sector in innovatively increasing the number of trunk gas pipes that could be carried on BDA bogie bolster wagon from five to six, as seen in this photograph taken early in 1980 at the loading point at Leith Docks near the ish Gas pipe coating installation. The trains were then destined to wherever in the U.K. the gas authorities were laying mains for the ribution of natural gas.

low: Modern VGA wagons were introduced on the Speedlink wagonload services. Two were being loaded at Inverness on 10th gust 1983.

Above: English Electric Co-Co No. 37 112 passes Elderslie on 9th October 1982 with a southbound bulk oil train from the Grangemouth oil refinery.

Speedlink

The major problem for freight profitability lay with wagonload traffic, that is traffic in full wagons, but not enough to make a full train load. Within the U.K., voices were adamant that we ought to be able at least to make siding-to-siding traffic pay. The Speedlink concept was based on this premise, but needed to avoid the crippling

costs of trains calling at marshalling yards at stages along their journeys. Instead, trains would be organised into sections from specific starting points, that would join up at key sidings for the trunk haul part of the journey before splitting off for different destinations. Sections could be exchanged between trains, too. The splitting and joining would be done by the train engines.

As Speedlink expanded, so did the salesmen's aspirations. Enthusiasm for getting lots of new wagonload traffic sen trip workings farther and farther afield to collect wagons until the costs of collectic and tripping began to display heavy loss that threatened the viability of the busine International traffic via the cross-chann train ferries came in ever-larger bogie vans and bulk carriers aimed at a multitude of destinations that still needed shunting and tripping. With the prosp of gold at the end of a future Channel Tunnel, it seemed that these traffics ha to be retained at all costs.

Trainload

MGR (merry-go-round) coal as a conce had emerged as a result of the Beeching plan. In the 1970s the Labour governme had put pressure on BR to expand the cc carrying network. Brush Traction had produced 135 class 56 locomotives in almost indecent haste to meet the expected demand. By the early 1980s cc was still a big and profitable business, b the decline in the size of the coal mining industry had to be matched by reductio in the operation of MGR trains.

Bulk and finished steel was normally carried on fleets of older BR bogie bolste wagons, many of which were updated b fitting with air brakes and more modern styles of bolster to secure the loads. The had been changes in the way the wagon were managed, one of which was the adoption on the ER of fixed formation trains. The system worked well, at a tin when loose wagon shunting was becoming the bane of efficient operatio BR also introduced many new air-brake steel-carrying wagons.

BR's bogie bulk oil tankers at 100 tons gross laden weight were larger than thos used on the European continent, and set the scene for heavy load haul in this country, using class 31s and 37s in pairs, class 47s singly at the practical limits of their electrical equipment.

With class 47 diesels being drafted in to haul these long oil trains, BR needed more freight power to take over MGR

Figure 8: BR freight train productivity - Average freight train load (tons)

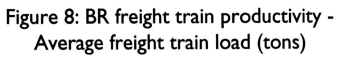
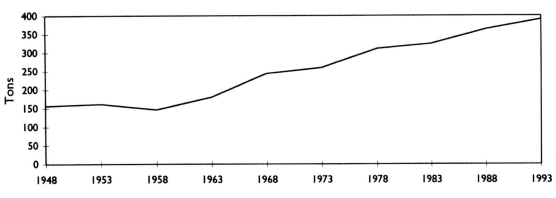

Figure 9: BR freight wagon productivity - Net ton miles per wagon in fleet

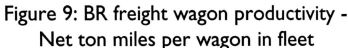
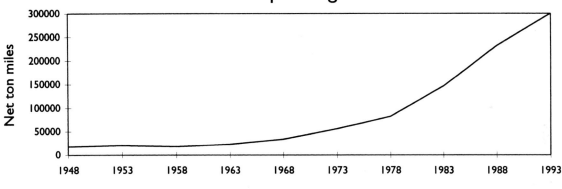

l, and designed the class 58, which ish built. Intended to be a simple, easy make Co-Co with export potential, the ss 58 had unusual looks, but was still a nventional British design reflecting tish understanding of what was ssible. In terms of tractive effort, the ss 58 made no real contribution to the ension of train loads or lengths yond what class 56s could haul. me of the most frightening substances be carried by train were handled by the chemicals sub-sector. For trains that carried hydrocyanic acid, for example, trains crews were, for a time, issued with protective equipment to be worn in the event of accident or derailment.

Road and motorway construction proceeded apace during the 1980s and demand for good stone appeared to be insatiable. Several wagon manufacturers produced designs of large bogie hopper wagons for aggregate companies across the country, particularly in Somerset and Derbyshire, who required BR to make long distance moves of large quantities of stone. The modern, air-braked, single product train was the ideal mechanism for this traffic.

Figures 8 and 9 show the huge strides BR made in improving freight train, and particularly wagon, productivity. Trainload freight became profitable under BR's firm business management.

The service sector

The service sector was not a business sector, but is a convenient term to use to describe the large fleets of ballast hopper wagons, rail carrying wagons and spoil wagons that the engineering departments owned for carrying loads that contributed to the maintenance of the railway. There were also fleets used by the M&E engineers, the overhead wiring trains being among them; and by the signal engineers for, among other things, stringing cables along the track for dropping into concrete troughs. Traditionally, these departmental wagons were regarded on the railway as of lower priority than the "commercial" fleet. Waiting lists of departmental wagons grew and the utilisation of the service fleets became poor. It would need an entirely new form of management organisation to resolve this long-term dilemma, which was to come, but not yet. END

Above: On 28th June 1986, a pair of English Electric Type 1 Bo-Bos led by No. 20 005 drift downhill near Chinley with a limestone train from Tunstead in Derbyshire to Northwich in Cheshire. The vacuum-braked bogie hopper wagons on this flow were mainly of pre-war construction, and privately-owned by ICI.

Top Left: Stone traffic developed quickly in the 1970s and 1980s as motorway and trunk road construction accelerated. Two BR/Sulzer Class 25 Bo-Bos head a train of Tilcon stone hoppers from Grassington to Hull at Broomfleet in 1975.

Bottom Left: Bulk grain wagons were a common sight on the east coast main line and the GN/GE joint line for many years. In May 1972 Class 40 1Co-Co1 No. 271 heads privately-owned empty grain wagons from Scotland to East Anglia through Doncaster. Later bulk grain trains utilised modern bogie "grainflow" hoppers.

The PTEs

MetroTrain

Another source of cash

Following the setting up by the Wilson Labour government of large regional local authorities covering the great conurbations, it was not long before BR was able to tap them as a source of subsidy income for local railways. In the early 1970s, Passenger Transport Authorities (PTAs) were set up in Greater Glasgow (later renamed Strathclyde on enlargement); Tyne & Wear; South-East Lancashire North East Cheshire (SELNEC), better known since renaming as Greater Manchester; Merseyside; West Yorkshire; West Midlands; and South Yorkshire. The PTAs were to determine passenger transport strategy for their areas. Reporting to them were Passenger Transport Executives (PTEs) who managed the year-by-year funding of railways and buses through a system known as Section 20 grants. The PTEs also took a strong lead in pressing BR to obtain better performance from their local services in all respects.

Right: The establishment of Passenger Transport Executives (PTEs) provided a local government source of funds for railway investment. Greater Glasgow PTE supported BR Scottish Region in re-opening after nearly 20 years the Glasgow Central Low Level route, linking the north-west Clyde suburban area with the south-east towns of Rutherglen, Motherwell and Hamilton. On 5th November 1979, a westbound train from Hamilton to Dumbarton Central formed by new thyristor-controlled electric multiple unit No. 314211 calls at Argyle Street station, newly constructed to feed the city's central shopping area.

Trains

The PTEs also began to play a leading role in rolling stock replacement. Greater Glasgow PTE funded BR's acquisition of the 16 class 314 thyristor-controlled electric multiple units to enable the newly reconstituted cross-city Argyle Line to be reopened after being closed for nearly twenty years. For Merseyrail, BR provided a new d.c. version of the same design of train, with a conventional control system, the class 507, to replace old LMS trains on the Liverpool-Southport run. Merseyrail later inherited from the Southern Region nearly-new class 508s that were virtually the same in design. These were used to splace the LMS and early BR Wirral line electric units.

...est Yorkshire PTE was instrumental, ...ong with Greater Manchester and Tyne ...d Wear, in funding BR's purchase of ...acer' type two-axle diesel multiple units ...r use around Leeds and Bradford, ...anchester, Newcastle and Teesside. In ...ne, these ceased to be popular units as

they compared unfavourably in ride and appointment with later d.m.u.s such as 'Sprinters', but at the time they were instrumental in causing increases in passenger carryings that greatly encouraged BR and the PTEs. West Midlands PTE supported the purchase of a small group of slam-door class 312 electric units for use around Birmingham.

Developments

During the 1980s there were many positive developments including several PTEs opening new stations on the lines they supported. West Yorkshire purchased their own 'Sprinter' diesel multiple units outright, unlike the normal method wherein sets were funded by PTEs but

Above: On 8th April 1989, West Midlands PTE held a gala day to publicise the opening of a new d.m.u. service from Walsall to Hednesford in Staffordshire. The day was over-subscribed, as seen from the crowd awaiting this class 114 unit arriving at the new platform at Hednesford.

owned by BR. In the West Yorkshire case, BR operated and maintained the PTE-owned train sets. In the 1990s, it was West Yorkshire that boldly proposed, and got, electrification of the Leeds and Bradford area suburban routes, having been most successful in raising passenger carryings on them over the previous two decades. Likewise, West Midlands secured electrification of their Cross-City route, with new class 323 e.m.u.s, and Greater Manchester PTE obtained new rail access to Manchester Airport.

I have never quite understood why the Cardiff valleys and other local communities in industrial South Wales did not warrant PTA status. True, there was no grand regional council to take the job on, but surely the local county councils could have managed it. After all, later, under

Above: West Yorkshire PTE went one step further than other PTEs by purchasing trains outright for BR to operate, as opposed merely to funding their purchase by BR. WYPTE first bought seven two-car class 155 'Sprinter' units, resplendent in their own maroon livery. This order was followed several years later by a batch of class 158 units, air-conditioned and capable of 90mph running. 158 903 poses in York station in May 1991.

rgaret Thatcher's Conservative govern-
nt, all the English regional councils were
lished and the counties had to take their
ce and collectively control the PTAs. In
s respect South Wales remains an
gma and an exception to an otherwise
cessful re-focusing of funding to
port positive railway developments in
big cities. This is not to under-value the
ellent work which the Glamorgan
horities did do in persuading BR to
pen lines and put in new stations, but a
th Wales PTE might have done it earlier
d with greater penetration in the valleys.

ke-overs

ile coming outside the scope of this
k, I should make brief mention of the
ne and Wear Metro light rail system and
Manchester Metrolink network. Both
k over former BR radial routes to feed

new cross-city routes, underground
through Newcastle and Gateshead, and
with on-street running in Manchester by
Metrolink tramcars.

Results

Was it all "deeply inefficient"? When I was
working in the Scottish Region from 1976
to 1984 I was aware repeatedly of efforts
by the PTE to improve services, make
better use of money, obtain better train
performance, reduce the Section 20
payments, and expand the supported
network. The PTE supported the refurbishment of the good old class 303

e.m.u.s, and would have gone for more
new stock had it been possible to justify at
the time. They rebuilt their own small
underground railway as a fine example of a
modern U-Bahn that became very much
more popular than before. Their positive,
forward-looking actions have enabled the
railway in their area to grow, while always
keeping on the pressure to contain or
reduce costs. It all depends how you
measure efficiency. If you asked
Strathclyde PTE what they thought of BR,
you would normally have got a positive
response. True, they were less happy at
times with the running of the old d.m.u.s
on the Ayr and Largs routes, but they
shared BR's view that only electrification

p Left: South Yorkshire PTE provided port for local services that radiated from ffield and Doncaster, many of which e worked by 'Pacer' units.

ttom Left: The MerseyRail network, ported by Merseyside PTE, included a nber of locations where PTE electric vices connected with separate diesel s. In this view at Kirkby on 16th May 34, the 11.00 class 108 d.m.u. from gan Wallgate (right) connects with a s 507 e.m.u. to Liverpool Central and nt's Cross.

ght: Tyne and Wear PTE not only ported BR diesel services in the wcastle area. It took over some routes, ed them through a new line under wcastle and Gateshead, and electrified m to form Britain's first light rail transit tro system. Unit 4069 arrives at South sforth on 21st March 1987 on a working t. James.

uld solve the reliability problems there, l put their money into the project, ich has been a great success.

ne PTEs were less fortunate at times. member reading that there have been casions when PTEs have threatened BR h withdrawal of some of their Section payments, an action open to all PTEs en dissatisfied with railway perfor-

mance. Interestingly, this has happened again after privatisation, so the term "deeply inefficient" could have been applied by politicians to the privatised operators, too. To discuss that, however, would be to trespass outside the timescale covered by this book. The chart in Figure 10 shows very clearly the reduction in total subsidy support for the

railway during the 1980s. The PTEs can take credit for much of this improvement. (In Figure 10, the apparently similar improvement noted after 1969 resulted partly from the restructuring of BR finances by the government.) ◆END◆

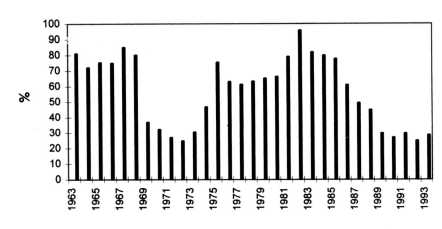

Figure 10: BR subsidy
% of passenger fares income

Down with regions

The businesses take over

Chapter 14 introduced the business culture, and showed how it was first used to develop marketing strategies and to define the services offered to railway customers. Moves soon took place to tighten the grip of the sectors on the railway even more completely. Chairman Sir Robert Reid's vision was of a railway that could balance the revenue received in any business sector with the expenditure necessary to run that sector and so show its "bottom line" clearly. Up to the introduction of the sectors, the only accurate bottom line had been that of the whole of BR.

The shrinking regions

The matrix organisation was described in chapter 14 as producing "constructive tensions" between the sectors, functions and the regions. In time, these tensions threatened to stall progress. They increased pressures on managers beyond what was then considered reasonable. It was logical that one group in the matrix had to go. In the face of the opposition of many managers, the decision was taken to dispense with the regions and that the businesses could more effectively manage the whole themselves, supported by the expertise of the BR HQ functions.

At that time I was in the LMR, the largest

Left: As the railway sectors became more accountable as businesses, they at last abandoned most aspects of BR's corporate image. In an early version of the InterCity livery, 25kV a.c. Bo-Bo No. 86 246 *Royal Anglian Regiment* heads the 20.30 to Norwich at Liverpool Street station on 21st May 1985. Electrification of the Norwich route had recently been completed.

Above: InterCity eliminated several electric locomotive duties by adopting push-pull working in East Anglia and on the west coast main line. In 1991, a west coast express formed of a 110mph mark 3 set was photographed at speed south of Berkhamsted on 17th September 1991.

Below: As a result of the BRB's manufacturing and maintenance policy study, the heavy repair shop at Stratford was used for a few years for diesel and electric locomotive over-hauls as well as dealing with major repairs. On 20th August 1987 No. 47 523 was being repaired in company with another class 47, a class 31 and a 37.

region of them all and the last to divest it workload. Because the HQ M&EE depa ment had had business divisions longer than other departments it was more read than most to absorb the work that the regions had done. In fact, work was divested both upwards to the M&EE bus ness engineers, and downwards (in organisational terms) to the area M&EEs Because the LMR was large, this set of changes was undertaken in stages. The first stage was elimination of the pos tion of regional M&E engineer (the forme regional CM&EE position), leaving the traction and rolling stock engineer and th electrification and plant engineer as the two top M&E engineers in the region. At the same time the regional M&E central staff were also disbanded, many people moving to the strengthened areas or to th BRB's M&EE HQ at the Railway Technic Centre in Derby. This was because tech-nical support for the railway businesses was to be undertaken by people at the RTC, not in the regions, while the areas would have technical people on site to handle day-to-day problems. Thus in my case I lost an LMR HQ team of some 80 people, but continued to have responsi-bility for the depots and the 2,000-odd sta

Above: One regional action that with hindsight appears not to have been in the best interests of the railway as a whole was the Scottish Region's decision to give the Forth Bridge a "maintenance holiday" for a year or two to save money. When repairs to the bridge were again needed, the old methods of access to the high girders were considered hazardous from a health and safety viewpoint. It took several years before a satisfactory method of maintaining the Forth Bridge could again be achieved.

Left: On 26th June 1985 class 455 e.m.u. No. 5743 calls at Clapham Junction bound for Dorking. The abolition of the Southern Region later that decade transferred all operating and maintenance personnel of the London BR areas to the London & South East sector.

Achievements

People had long told me that the LM region was so big as to be unmanageable, but I found that, as soon as I no longer had to manage the 80-strong former regional HQ traction and rolling stock group, I had much more time to concentrate on supporting and monitoring the areas and depots. My electrification and plant colleague and I developed with the area engineers a team spirit such as we had not had before. We made considerable progress in the eighteen months in which this slimmed organisation was intact. Figures from the 1986 to 1988 period show that in the last years of the LM region we improved reliability and availability of diesel and electric locomotives substantially, changed for all time the concept of carriage interior cleaning and condition, and reduced by nearly half the minutes delay debited to traction and rolling stock in the LM's performance monitoring system. They showed that not even the LMR was totally unmanageable!

...thin them. To help me do this I had a ...ff of five senior engineers, then shortly ...be relocated from Derby to Birmingham ...join all other LM regional HQ staff (apart ...m the operators who were at Crewe).

Above: Railfreight in the Nottinghamshire and Yorkshire coal fields had to behave almost as though regional boundaries did not exist. The power stations alongside the River Trent were in the ER and the LMR, and the coal supplies came from both regions, too. The logic of devolving management to one business was sound. At Toton yard class 58 Co-Co No. 58 036 had arrived on 17th September 1991 with a trip working carrying coal in HDA hoppers at the front, and HAA (MGR) wagons at the rear.

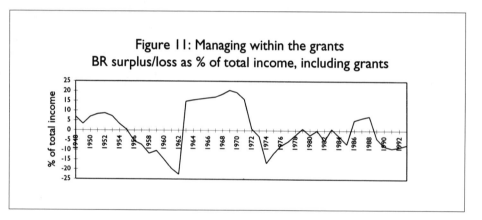

Regions go

By early 1989, all the regions had closed down. I jointly chaired a somewhat strained meeting of over 200 people at Blackpool at which we consulted with t staff representatives about the necessar changes to enable the LM region's M&E areas and depots to reorganise and to w under the HQ M&E business engineers retrospect, it seems to me that we under took those changes in considerable hast Thankfully, due to the innate determina tion of railwaymen to do the best for the individual bit of railway, the changeove took place successfully, albeit painfully some people.

Safety

Late in 1988, three trains had collided in cutting near Clapham Junction, London The subsequent, independent inquiry resulted in BR adopting a whole new culture of managed safety. The emphas began to change from the old method of attaining safety by just learning lessons from the last accident. BR had to learn ne techniques such as risk management and the systematic management of change. Life on Britain's railways was changing for good. ◄END►

Left: The successful introduction of the business philosophy on British Rail was t result of the vision and drive of the then chairman of BRB, Sir Robert Reid (centre He was rewarded with the knowledge th large parts of the railway at that time were heading for subsidy-free operation *Brian Morrison*

Right Supported by Greater Manchester PTE, 25kV e.m.u. No. 303 060 approaches Dinting level crossing on 24th December 1984 with a service to Glossop and Hadfie

Towards privatisation: phoney

Businesses in ascendancy

The strong BR HQ departments were always going to be more difficult to dismantle than the regions, and so it proved. By early 1989 the regions had gone. The railways were managed by the businesses who had by then allocated all stretches of railway line to one or another of their kind. The business that "owned" a particular railway route paid for the infrastructure costs of that route in full as "prime user".

s there was pressure for a business to get
[of] routes that were either very costly, or
[whi]ch could, by relinquishing prime user
[stat]us, be passed on to another business to
[pay] for. This happened to many BR lines,
[clas]sic cases being parts of the Leeds to
[Car]lisle route and the Gloucester-Newport
[line] via Chepstow where Railfreight and
[Inter]City respectively opted out completely
[leav]ing those routes for Regional Railways
[(as] Other Provincial Services had become
[kno]wn) to pay for. Another was the extrac-
[tion] by Regional Railways from the Dore
[sout]h curve, by dint of running all their
[Not]tingham-Manchester trains into
[She]ffield and reversing. That put the cost of
[the] Dore curve fully on to Railfreight, but
[pre]vented subsequent flexibility in
[mar]keting fast regional passenger services,
[ad]ding some 20 minutes to all through
[jour]neys. The prime user principle also
[app]lied to use of stations, sidings and yards.
[Aft]er the new businesses had firmly

established themselves, the former three
M&E business engineers had become
five, there being one business engineer
supporting each business. The train

maintenance depots became individually
dedicated to a business where this was
practicable. In the many cases where
several businesses shared a depot, the

Top Left: When Chris Green took over L&SE as managing director he re-branded the system 'Network SouthEast' and launched a new, bold house style. The new class 442 five-car e.m.u.s for the Bournemouth and newly electrified Weymouth services carried the NSE livery, as seen on unit 2421 passing Vauxhall on 18th October 1995 on the 13.30 from Waterloo to Bournemouth and Weymouth. Towards the end of this phase of BR's life, NSE was heading towards eventual profitability, subject to the economy staying on course, which it did not!

Bottom Left: The parcels business was also rebranded, taking the name 'Rail express systems' (Res). The single Gloucester d.m.u. parcels van No. 55991 photographed at York on 1st March 1990 carries the older red livery that was used to denote vehicles carrying Royal Mail traffic. The Res livery was also red, and presented an image of a business that actually cared about carrying parcels for its customers.

Below: The second and third generations of 'Sprinters', classes 155, 156 and 158, raised the passenger comfort standard of diesel multiple units above the accepted norm. The 156s, and the 158s that followed them, enabled Regional Railways (as Provincial Services had become) to confound the sceptics with new cross-country routes linking the west and east of the country with short, regular interval trains which helped to stabilise the sector's earnings. On one such service, from Liverpool to Ipswich, unit 156 403 calls at Nottingham.

Above: The greatest project BR completed in the 1980s was the east coast route electrification, finished on time and within its forecast budget. Designed for 140mph operation, and so dubbed 'InterCity 225' (225km/h = 140mph), the class 91-hauled mark 4 train sets were immediately popular, particularly after early carriage riding troubles on the Swiss bogies had been sorted out by the engineers. No. 91 006 arrives at Leeds City on 7th March 1990 with the 09.10 from London King's Cross.

Right: As an autonomous business, wholly owned by BR and no longer receiving government subsidy, InterCity's new branding retained the basic two-tone grey train colours but used a quality lettering style supported by the swallow symbol. This is the 06.30 Plymouth to Newcastle HST arriving at Cheltenham on 14th August 1989.

guest businesses became customers of the prime user of the depot. The other engineering functions had new customers, too: the businesses that were the prime users of the railways in their territory. The businesses themselves managed railway sales, marketing, train operations, strategic planning and customer service.

Having got the costs of managing the infrastructure and train fleets tied into internal contracts, BR was at last in a position to know the bottom line of each of its businesses, and was able much better to assess the value of investment proposals. Henceforth, orders for new rolling stock, for example, would be based on a clear case for improvements in revenue or reduction in known costs, or more usually a combination of both.

Boom times for some

When John Edmunds moved upwards out of the London & South East chair, Chris Green replaced him and quickly stamped on the whole organisation his confident approach to selling railway travel. He relaunched L&SE as Network SouthEast in a blaze of publicity with new, colourful train liveries that were part of an overall business identity that led to red lamp posts everywhere, re-signing at all stations and a feeling among railway staff that at last they had a railway that served all London.

The rise of the sectors on BR came at a time of national economic expansion. Passenger carryings rose dramatically, carrying more traffic on the reduced, post-Beeching network than had been carried in the years before the route closures. InterCity became

profitable, and Network SouthEast show a trend that would have reached profitability had not the economy turned dow when the Lawson boom went bust. Freight continued to dribble away, even after BR had long since got out of wagonload traffic. There was an attempt revive wagonload distribution with the Speedlink network. Eventually the cost o tripping wagons to and from distant traffi sources to join the trunk trains overcame

y hope of making wagonload pay and
eedlink was abandoned. Railfreight was
lit between the train load business, to be
own as Trainload Freight, and the rest,
ilfreight Distribution (RfD).
e confidence in the Parcels sector was
lected in a relaunch of that business
der the "Rail express systems" name.
e red train liveries continued with
odification, and there was much invest-
ent in improvements to bogie rail vans to
enable use of modern loading and
unloading systems with fork lift trucks and
containerisation.

The Freightliner trains, staff, depots and
lorries had been off-loaded from BR to be a
subsidiary of National Freight Corporation,
a road-based group, only to be re-absorbed
into BR a decade or so later as part of RfD.
Following the sale of station catering to the
private sector, train catering became a
wholly owned BR subsidiary known as On
Board Services (OBS). BR Research, and the
many former M&EE teams at the RTC that
had not already been drawn into the
passenger or freight train businesses, were
grouped under the umbrella of a commer-
cially-oriented company called Central
Services. Central Services also took over
management of the service train fleet,
bringing for the first time in railway history a
higher level of priority to that activity.
Probably the most exciting wholly-owned

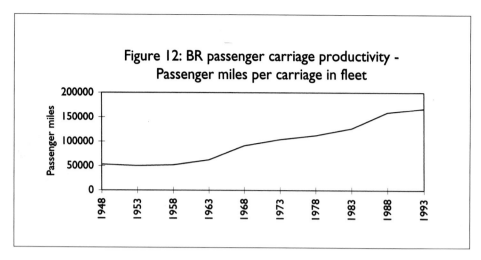

Figure 12: BR passenger carriage productivity - Passenger miles per carriage in fleet

company was the European Passenger Services (EPS) company set up within BR to manage BR's share in Eurostar train procurement and operation in readiness for the opening of the Channel Tunnel. outcome of this company's activities, w project responsibility taken by BR's maj projects division, was the design and construction of Waterloo International station. That very fine building was read on time and within budget for a 1992 service start date which the private secto Eurotunnel and train supplier teams missed by more than a year. That was th same major projects division that earlier had led the electrification of the east coa main line to its on-time completion, also within its budget. This hardly merited t description of a "deeply inefficient" nationalised industry!

This was a period of relative financial stability for BR when compared with the see-saw years of the 1948 to 1974 period Figure 11 shows how BR managed to kee its year end results within less than 10% the annual objective in its last two decades. In this graph, numbers "above the line" represent years in which at least an operating profit was made. In later years any such profits were clawed back by the government on the grounds that a lower net subsidy resulted. Numbers "below the line" in Figure 11 show losses incurred after BR had received and accounted for all subsidies.

Towards privatisation?

The idea that British Rail would be privatised was being formulated for several years before the final scheme was developed. Having divided BR up into a number of clearly defined and costed bu nesses with their own bottom lines, and with contracts in place that controlled their relationships with internal supplier such as the engineering functions, we could identify a possible set of privatisab railway businesses. We believed that tha was what we were doing, and we worked wholeheartedly to make it all work. The second Sir Bob Reid played a significant sometimes unsung role in the evolution.

uality

ring the "organisation for quality"
Q) reorganisation that had led to the
siness structure of BR, the heavy
olvement of some senior managers and
gineers in the change process had the
ential to "take their eyes off the ball"
ofar as concerned the continuing
cess of squeezing costs out of the
way. The regions had been good at that
the businesses were poised ready to
ke further inroads into costs with their
ter focus. However, circumstances
re shortly to change radically and were
ocus more management time on yet
re change rather than on on-going
provements to the railways. I believe
t BR reached its peak of efficient and
ective operations in the late 1980s and
ly 1990s. The sweeping changes that
owed, leading to the privatisation we
w have, form a complex and in many
ys a positive story, but one which
nnot be written in full or objectively at
time of writing because the medium
m effects are yet to come. ◼END◼

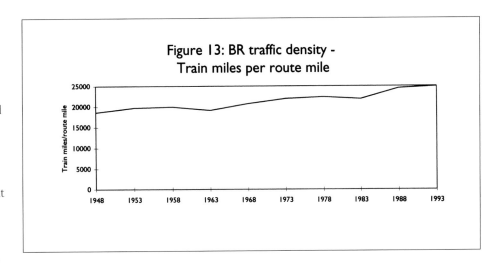

Figure 13: BR traffic density -
Train miles per route mile

p Left: New trains were purchased by
for Strathclyde PTE services. E.m.u. No.
0 303 arrives at Partick on a north Clyde
orking to Drumgelloch on 30th July 1992.
ese units were similar to the class 321s
at Network SouthEast was buying for
rth of London services.

ttom Left: Trainload Freight no longer
lied on government subsidy for its opera-
ns. Class 56 Co-Co No. 56 108
proaches Duffield north of Derby with an
npty train of steel carrying wagons bound
Sheffield on 8th February 1996.

Towards privatisation: real

Options

Any government seeking ways to privatise its state-owned railways has many options from which to decide its preferred method. The British Thatcher government, for example had initially encouraged BR's split into clearly defined businesses, several of which had become wholly-owned companies. This led people within BR to believe that they were moulding the privatised railway of the future. Soon, all that would have to be done would be to offer the various existing parts for sale as individual companies. Large though many of these BR businesses were, they were readily manageable when compared with the much larger utilities that the government had already embarked on selling, such as British Gas and British Telecom. Indeed, the sale of complete railways was the pattern adopted by South American countries such as Argentina, and followed the American ideal of large, vertically integrated railway companies. By "vertically integrated" I mean that the railway owns everything from the trackbed and signalling upwards to the trains and staff that operate and maintain them. It would

Right: The major investment for Network SouthEast was the purchase of the large fleet of Networker e.m.u.s which enabled slam door inner suburban stock to be eliminated from the South Eastern business. These class 465s were expensive units, with eight traction motors per four-car set and with regenerative braking so that on deceleration the trains could put current back into the third rail. This is No. 465 204 stabled at Strawberry Hill depot before its introduction to service.

have been possible through legislation to set up a regulatory body to ensure that the interests of the population were kept high on the railways' agenda.

Dividing up BR into geographically distinct railways such as the old GWR or LNER would have been almost impossible, and the existing division into railway businesses was at least a tenable alternative.

produce more meaningful comparisons of railway costs and revenues with those of other forms of transport.

The British government's response under prime minister John Major was to go even further than the directive required, namely completely to split off the management of infrastructure from the management of train operations.

Above: As BR prepared for privatisation, the Freightliner organisation was separated out from Railfreight Distribution for sale as free-standing business. Freightliners Limite later became part of the English, Welsh & Scottish Railway (EWS) that also owned al of what had once been Trainload Freight a Rail express systems. On 27th May 1988, 4 397 passes Woking with a down Freightlin train for Southampton with containers of deep-sea traffic.

European directive

The impact of European Directive 440/91 on the railways of Europe has been mixed. The key issue for our discussion is the requirement that financial accounts for the costs and revenues attributed to railway operations should be separate from those for railway infrastructure. This was to enable a clearer understanding to emerge of the actual costs of providing each railway route, and to

Railtrack

Thus was conceived the formation of Railtrack, initially as a wholly-owned company within British Rail. At the same time, the Adam Smith Institute and others were asked to consider how best to split up British Rail including Railtrack into saleable units.

Railtrack was to inherit the track, structures, buildings, signalling and signal control functions from the BR railway

businesses. Railtrack was to be divided u into ten geographically identifiable zone that would manage the railway infrastru ture within their areas including the lettin of contracts for maintenance and renewa and which would undertake day-to-day train control. Each zonal director would report directly to Railtrack's chief executive who in turn reported to the chairman so reporting lines were kept short. The zones were in most respects fully

tonomous units, that could if necessary
bsequently be sold as individual railway
frastructure units.

rain operations

on't think that anyone working in the
dustry at that time expected the develop-
ent of the train operating units (TOUs) to
sult in so many as twenty-five passenger
hits. The TOUs were set up as wholly-
vned companies within BR. They were
be sold into the private sector as fran-
ises, not owning rolling stock or
ations, so in effect their only key assets, at
ast at the start, would be people.
he job of the franchisee, therefore,
ould be to offer a train service that
ould attract customers and earn revenue
hile managing costs so that the bottom
ne came out as a profit. From the start
e government would pay agreed subsi-
es which would usually be on a
ducing basis through the life of the fran-
ise, thus forcing the operator to
prove its efficiency year by year. The
yments would be enacted through the
fice of the passenger rail franchising
rector (OPRAF).
further the concept of competition, BR
eated three freight companies out of
ainload Freight, which gained the names
LoadHaul, Mainline Freight, and
ansrail. These had a geographic basis for
e split but would penetrate each others'
rritories as traffic developed. Unlike the
assenger companies, the freight compa-
es would own their rolling stock from
e beginning, except for the many
agons that were already privately owned
hirers and customers and which already
rried a substantial proportion of the
ation's railway freight.
eightliners Ltd. came away from its brief
ay within Railfreight Distribution (RfD)
d became a saleable company in its own
ght. RfD was burdened by the unpre-
cted, slow growth of Channel Tunnel
eight volume and BR put its sale on the
ack burner for a year or two.
y the mid 1990s Rail express systems
es) had established itself as a successful
rrier with a modern train fleet, at least in

Above: New class 323 e.m.u.s were purchased by BR for West Midlands PTE, by then operating under the Centro name. They were the first a.c. e.m.u.s to be accepted for all-network operation under the new Railtrack acceptance system. 323 204 calls at Gravelly Hill on 4th November 1997 with the 11.01 from Longbridge to Lichfield City.

Below: Railfreight Distribution aimed to be in a position to accept the forecast growth of Channel Tunnel traffic. On a day when traffic was quiet, 47 525 takes a single international bogie van northbound through Leicester on 17th September 1997. RfD was to be the last railway business to be sold by BR, in 1997.

ms of the up-to-date parcels handling
uipment and its refurbished fleet. Its
ss 47s gained new levels of reliability
e to the dedicated work of its central
ewe depot, and its fleet of smart if
eing red-and-black trains reflected for
e first time ever that someone on the
lway did not regard parcels as a
nderella traffic.

assenger Rolling Stock

r two weeks early in 1994 I assisted BR's
ndor unit in formulating outline
oposals for leasing passenger rolling
ock. The majority of our recommenda-
ons were accepted by the British
ilways Board and the government.
ey led directly to the establishment of
ee rolling stock leasing companies
OSCOs) with life long responsibility for
e engineering condition of the vehicles
their fleets.
e names of the ROSCOs - Angel,
ersholt and Porterbrook - became as
uch railway household names as were
eat Western, BREL and Travellers Fare.

ESCOs

hought it a bit corny when the acronym
ESCO was adopted for the train engi-
eering service companies. Three of these
ere set up within BR to absorb the work
rried out by the former business engin-
rs' rolling stock technical staff at the
TC. Interfleet took on the work covering
terCity type vehicles, Network Train
ngineering were the experts in e.m.u.s,
d The engineering **link** took on d.m.u.s
d freight locomotives and wagons.
ey soon began to compete with each
her in areas well outside the boundaries
their original expertise.

Railway safety

he major debate in the popular press and
the railways was over how such a
smembered railway system could retain
good a safety record as had BR before it.

Above: A pioneer business set up within BR was European Passenger Services (EPS) which had the task of preparing the British share of the Eurostar Channel Tunnel train service, together with its partners, SNCF and SNCB. A Eurostar train formed of units 3226 and 3225 forming the 12.13 from Paris Nord to London Waterloo passes Ashford International station on the up through line at speed on 3rd June 1996.

Left: Privately-owned wagons have run on Britain's railways for most of this century, with a partial respite after nationalisation. From 1985, privately owned locomotives began to operate on freight, in the form of Foster Yeoman and ARC class 59 General Motors Co-Cos. The class 59s introduced to this country the concept of slow speed creep control giving very high tractive effort. This facility was incorporated in BR's own class 60, 100 of which were purchased from Brush from 1989 to 1993. ARC No. 59 101 was photographed passing Wandsworth Road station on 27th August 1996 with empty stone hoppers.

Safety was possibly the one overriding issue that caused Railtrack to be sold as a monopoly infrastructure company rather than each zone being sold separately. The overall responsibility for railway safety was vested in Railtrack as the infrastructure owner and operator. Critical to the safety regime's success would be the relationships between Railtrack and its contractors, and the train operators and their suppliers.

Railtrack set up a directorate for safety and standards, reporting straight to the chairman so as to be fully independent of the operating part of Railtrack. I was a member of the project team that designed the standards process and which coined the now-familiar term Railway Group Standards.

The regime of safety standards led to the principle that each operator had to have a railway safety case (RSC) approved by Railtrack before being considered to be a competent and safe operator. In its RSC an operator had to demonstrate what its safety system was and how the company managed it. No safety case would be approved unless the operator had robust arrangements to ensure that its own suppliers (of rolling stock, spare parts, people, equipment, fuel, etc.) were themselves not going to be a risk to railway

Above: The first privately owned multipl[e]
units to run on BR were the class 325 dual
voltage e.m.u.s purchased by Royal Mail fo[r]
their national mail distribution system.
Royal Mail based the network on a new hu[b]
depot at Wembley and sited smaller mail
handling depots strategically throughout
the country. No. 325 011 was at Crewe
station on 4th November 1997 being
loaded for a southbound run on the west
coast main line.

Left: Towards the end of BR the Board
made a dictat that there should be no new
train liveries in view of the likelihood that
the private owners would want to apply
their own. An exception was made for the
Thameslink trains, which were all becomin[g]
due for repainting and for which, it was sai[d]
NSE colours would be unsuitable. The gre[y]
livery with large maroon insignia had sprea[d]
to half the class 319 fleet before the franchisee decided on a new style anyway! Th[is]
unit was pictured at Farringdon, the statio[n]
where changeover is made between d.c.
and a.c. operation.

ety. New or modified traction and
[roll]ling stock would also have to pass
[thr]ough a detailed process of safety accep-
[tan]ce to ensure its integrity on the railway.

[C]ontractors

[Ra]iltrack intended not to own the means
[of] repairing and developing its railway
[tra]ck and infrastructure systems. The
[wo]rk of maintaining the track, signalling
[an]d buildings went to a group called BRIS
[(Br]itish Rail Infrastructure Services) which
[wa]s split up into infrastructure mainte-
[na]nce units (IMUs) and track repair units
[(T]RUs). These teams individually
[con]tracted with the Railtrack zones to
[un]dertake the physical work on main-
[tai]ning and improving the network. The
[IM]Us and TRUs were later turned into
[ind]ividual wholly-owned companies
[rea]dy for selling to the outside world.

[B]ottom lines

[Th]e new arrangements appeared at first
[sig]ht to be extremely complex, and indeed
[so]me commentators viewed the whole
[ass]embly as potentially hazardous. The
[saf]ety relationships were however signifi-
[can]tly more robust than those which BR
[ha]d had in place before, as a result of the
[re]al scrutiny they underwent as part of
[the] pre-privatisation process.
[Ra]iltrack would adopt a system of track
[acc]ess charges that would reflect the
[am]ount of use the operators made of
[spe]cific routes and the volume of their
[tra]ffic. In effect, Railtrack sold train paths
[to] the operators.
[In] their turn, the train operators would pay
[lea]sing charges for their trains to the
[ow]ning ROSCOs, who would contract
[wi]th firms like BREL and BRML (who were
[als]o sold) for their overhaul work. The
[op]erators would manage their own day-
[to-]day train maintenance using depots
[wh]ich they would lease from Railtrack but
[wh]ich they would staff and control them-
[sel]ves. Thus every company out of the
[100]-odd involved would know the cost of
[wh]at it was doing, and would have a

source of income through its contracts
with other companies from which to
construct a bottom line.
An overseeing eye was needed to take into
account the needs of the general public
and other railway customers, and to
ensure that the government got value for
its money. This role was given to the
Railway Regulator.
By the time of the May 1997 election, all BR
including Railtrack had been sold with the
notable exception of Railfreight
Distribution, disposal of which was in
hand. It is not for this book to chronicle the
results of privatisation of Britain's railways.
That is for a book that cannot sensibly be
written until the earliest franchises have
reached maturity and have been through
the seven-year resale process, or whatever
other process the government of that day
decides is appropriate. ■END■

Above: Railfreight Distribution and SNCF
obtained a fleet of Co-Co class 92 dual-
voltage locomotives for operation of
Channel Tunnel freight trains. The complex
nature of their electronics caused them to
fall foul of Railtrack's acceptance processes,
but by the time of RfD's sale in summer
1997 most had been passed to work
between Calais and Wembley yard.
No. 92 024 *J S Bach* heads north through
Kensington Olympia on 12th January 1998
with an intermodal Channel Tunnel train
carrying lorry swap-bodies from Italy to
northern U.K.

A new future?

I had originally intended this chapter to be entitled 'Valedictory' as if BR were in effect dead. It was to chart the results of BR's work in making its railway system an effective one when compared with others in the world, and indeed it still does that. But BR is not dead. The Blair government in 1997 gave the BRB a new role, to chart the strategic future for Britain's railway system taking into account the New Labour aim of an integrated transport system for the country. As the body which formerly ran a "deeply inefficient" railway system according to the previous prime minister, was this a wise choice for the Blair government to make to carry out this task?

The answer to that question underlines the key issue that threads through this book. To be considered a deeply inefficient railway, BR would have to compare badly with railway systems elsewhere that are known to be efficient. Leeds University undertook two attempts at such a comparison, using other western European railways as benchmarks. At the beginning of the 1980s BR was in the middle of the bunch, well ahead of Belgium and Italy but far behind such high-flyers as the Netherlands and Sweden. By the early 1990s the position had changed dramatically. BR was ahead of or level with the most efficient railways according to most

Right: When the west coast main line franchise was sold to Virgin Trains, the company made very bold forecasts as to how much extra traffic they could take by replacing the present InterCity trains with new tilting trains running on a rebuilt railway. In the author's opinion, the west coast main line at the end of BR's tenure offered a good, comfortable product, typical of which is this mark 3 push-pull set speeding through Leighton Buzzard forming the 07.05 service from Glasgow Central to London Euston on 17th September 1991. One views the future with muted excitement!

Above: Former Railfreight Distribution class 90 Bo-Bo electric No. 90 136 approaches Bletchley with a northbound Channel Tunnel freight on 2nd February 1998. The present operators of most of Britain's freight services, EWS, aim to treble freight carryings over the next few years, making maximum use of the opportunity for expanding international workings. To cope with this, Railtrack is studying additional routes around London, one of which could bring into frequent use (for the first time!) the Bletchley flyover that takes the Tonbridge-Reading-Oxford orbital route over the west coast main line. Again, one views the prospects of such heavy traffic with excitement.

of the different measures used. Since that review, of course, there has been the hiatus in management's efforts to improve the railway, caused by the diversion of so much management time to the changes necessary to prepare for the privatisation which we now have. During that time, BR's efficiency probably dropped a little, partly as a result of the national recession and BR's inability to keep pace with the drop in revenue that ensued at the same time as everything else it was doing.

Commentators have made much of the perceived cost to the taxpayer of the privatised railway being much greater than that of BR before it was split up, almost double

in fact. I put this down to two things. Firstly, as I have already said, detailed cost-cutting within BR slowed down during the privatisation process. The second reason is more fundamental. BR and the regions used to struggle through periods of revenue crisis and government cut-backs by holding back on non-critical investment in order to sustain the operating railway and balance their books. Railtrack's remit, in contrast, requires it to sustain investment in stations, track, structures and signalling virtually irrespective of the financial performance of the train operators, to recover the "maintenance backlog" and provide a railway system capable of meeting the needs of the future. BR was

not specifically mandated to do that. So the rules have changed substantially. The ability of the government to turn off the railway investment tap when times a tough has been thwarted for the foreseeable future, which cannot be a bad thing. But that stability has to be paid for, and th increased open subsidy that the sum of t payments to franchisees represents has t be higher than before, at least at first. As the years go by, the reduced payments th the government makes through OPRAF its successor will tighten the screws and make the taxpayer's burden less.

This book, as any reader who has read th far will have decided, concludes that British Rail as latterly constituted was by no means "deeply inefficient". Indeed, despite the heavy hand of government with its own short-term financial manipu latory needs, BR reached as high a state o efficiency as any national railway system in Europe, an achievement of which it an the nation may remain pleased. This wa achieved without the undoubted stimulu of private ownership and enterprise.

ow the railways of Britain face a new era
th opportunities to become even more
icient than was BR. In the years after
vatisation there will be profitable
mpanies and there may be some failures.
the course of time there may be changes
ownership, mergers and take-overs as
e shape of the railway industry evolves.
ish them all well in what could probably
come another golden age of rail. **END**

p Right: Future suburban trains are
ely to be technically less complex than the
etworkers. Train procurement has
anged from building to the purchaser's
tailed design, to being offered from a
nge of suppliers' products. By contracting
e suppliers to undertake service provision
ring the life of a franchise, simpler, more
liable trains are likely to result.
etworker No. 465 016 was
otographed passing Wandsworth Road
26th April 1996.

Above: BR sold EPS with its Eurostar trains to London & Continental Railways, the consortium charged with building the high speed link between the Tunnel and London. A further change of ownership is expected at the time of writing (spring 1998). In this picture at the award-winning Waterloo International station, passengers are joining a Brussels-bound Eurostar service.

Bibliography

[1] *British Transport Commission First Annual Report, Statement of Accounts and Statistics* published in 1949 by Her Majesty's Stationery Office.

[2] Extracted from Appendix 1 of *BR Steam in Colour 1948-1968* by Colin Boocock, published in 1986 by Ian Allan Ltd, ISBN 0 7110 1671 2.

[3] The author's book *Railway Liveries BR Steam 1948-1968* published in 1989 by Ian Allan Ltd., ISBN 0 7110 1856 1, gives definitive descriptions of the railway liveries adopted for steam traction and associated rolling stock of British Railways.

[4] Details of the traction fleet introduced as a result of the modernisation plan are given in the author's book *British Railways in Colour* published in 1988 by Ian Allan Ltd., ISBN 0 7110 1767 0.

[5] R.H.N. Hardy's book *Beeching - Champion of the Railway?* was published by Ian Allan Ltd. in 1989, ISBN 0 7110 1855. It is a definitive biography that establishes a balanced perspective on Dr. (later Lord) Beeching's achievements as chairman of the British Railways Board, as well as giving a deep insight into the management of British Railways during that phase of its existence.

[6] *The Reshaping of British Railways (Part 1: Report; Part 2: Maps)* was published in 1963 by Her Majesty's Stationery Office.

[7] During preparation of the maps in this book, reference was made to the following publications: *The Reader's Digest Great World Atlas, 1968*; *British Railways Sectional Maps*, Ian Allan Ltd., ca. 1950; *Sectional Maps of Britain's Railways*, Ian Allan Ltd., 1982, ISBN 0 7110 1257 1; and *European Railway Atlas, British Isles*, second revised edition by M.G. Ball, Ian Allan Ltd. 1996, ISBN 0 7110 2407 3.

[8] *The development of the major trunk routes*, was published by the British Railways Board in 1965.

[9] These details are taken from *ScotRail* by Colin Boocock, published in 1986 by Ian Allan Ltd., ISBN 0 7110 1567.

[10] In *Transport Policy - An opportunity for change*, published by the British Railways Board in 1976, chairman Sir Richard Marsh makes the statement, "I doubt whether the railway will ever produce a conventional commercial return on cap[ital] invested and, indeed, I know of no railw[ay] in the world that does."

Below: The class 156 'Super-Sprinters' raised the standard of comfort for Region[al] Railways' customers and began the proce[ss] of revitalising non-InterCity cross-countr[y] travel. No. 156 408 heads along the Hop[e] Valley in Derbyshire near Earl's sidings on 7th May 1989 with an afternoon train fro[m] East Anglia to Liverpool.

British Railways in 1994